TIMELINES OF NATIVE AMERICAN HISTORY

Carl Waldman

Illustrated by Molly Braun

Designed by Robert Engle

Produced by TD Media, Inc.

Prentice Hall General Reference
15 Columbus Circle, New York, New York 10023

ISBN 0–671–88992–3
Interior designed by Robert Engle
Manufactured in Hong Kong
10 9 8 7 6 5 4 3 2 1
First Edition

HOW TO USE THIS BOOK

Native American history is North American history (as well as South American history) and central to the tradition of all Americans. Yet few dates from American Indian history are widely known, unless, like 1492, they are also part of the dominant Euroamerican tradition. The year 1890, when the U.S. army struck ferociously at Indian families camped along Wounded Knee Creek, has become a watershed date. The Battle of Little Bighorn in 1876 is also a familiar date, although for many its interest lies more in its significance to U.S. military history than to Indian history.

Timelines of Native American History attempts to provide an accessible view of many more events and dates from the Indian story. Native peoples have their own calendar systems for recording events, such as the "winter counts" of Kiowas and Sioux. Or a month might be referred to as "Moon when the Cold Makes the Trees Crack," a Lenni Lenape name for December. Each tribe merits its own published chronology of events in its own terms. These timelines, while struggling against the relentless thrust of Eurocentricism, are designed to complement public education as we now know it. So, even with Native American history as the subject matter, events and dates from the Euroamerican tradition must serve as the signposts. Public education has failed to emphasize that "progress," "growth," or the "opening of the frontier" has meant something else for American Indians. The adverse impact on native peoples and cultures should be inferred throughout *Timelines*.

The timelines are organized as follows:
- The **Culture** timeline relates Native American cultural developments, such as in subsistence, arts, religion, and education.
- The **Warfare & Protest** timeline includes Indian-white wars and Indian involvement in tribal and non-Indian wars, as well as political activism.
- The **Politics & Law** timeline shows political and legal events relevant to Native American history.
- A fourth, separate chronology, **European and Euroamerican Contacts with Native Americans**, is provided below the others as an additional frame of reference, giving dates of non-Indian exploration and settlement, along with Indian-white trade relationships. (In this instance, Euroamerican history is a footnote to Native American history rather than the opposite.)
- Different centuries are represented by different colors within the three timelines in order to align and compare the subject matter.

A **Chronology of Native American Prehistory** begins on page 3 of the book section. The Indian story of course did not begin with the European discovery of North America. (Using that date as a starting point in Indian studies is another example of Eurocentricism.) The prehistoric dates are largely hypothetical;

scholars are not in complete agreement as to early migrations and the time periods of particular cultures. Ongoing archaeological discoveries are changing long-held views.

The book section also includes a **Biographical Dictionary** (page 5) of Native Americans mentioned in the timelines; a list of **Famous Battles and Incidents** (page 17), providing additional details for events mentioned in the timelines; and a **Glossary of Cultural Terms** (page 21). Many of the terms in the glossary are based on the illustrations, as described in the list of **Captions & Credits** (page 29).

Throughout the timelines and in the book section, the names of states and provinces are used as points of reference even before statehood or provincial status was achieved.

The back panels of the timelines contain maps of the **Culture Areas of North America**. A "culture area" is a cartographic classification based on geography and customs. That is to say, geography, climate, and wildlife determined the way different peoples lived: what foods they ate, what materials they used for shelter and clothing, and how they viewed the world. "California Indians" of course had a much different way of life than "Subarctic Indians." Such a system also helps in generalizing Native American historical studies. One can say for example that many "Southeast Indians" were relocated westward in the 1830s, or that when the Spanish brought horses to North America in the 16th century, it began shaping a new "Plains Indian" way of life. (The Mesoamerican and Circum-Caribbean culture areas, sometimes included in North American Indian studies, are not depicted here. And the southern extents of the Southwest and California culture areas, part of Mexico, are also not shown.) On the maps, the location of tribes at about the time of contact with Europeans and Euroamericans are approximately given. It should be kept in mind that the time of first contacts between Indians and whites varied from region to region, that some tribes were extinct before extensive contacts, that some tribal locations shifted soon after early contacts, and that some among these peoples were nomadic within a much larger area than shown. Nor is every tribe or subtribe depicted cartographically. Some important battles, corresponding to the list in the book section, are also shown on a separate map. Present-day boundary lines of states and provinces are depicted for reference purposes.

As an outline, timelines serve to correlate different types of information, and are designed as starting points or reference tools for more in-depth studies. The book section provides a more detailed level of information. A **Bibliography** (page 31) of select titles will help the researcher delve deeper into the Indian saga and legacy.

CHRONOLOGY OF NATIVE AMERICAN PREHISTORY

c. before 15,000 B.C. (possibly as early as 50,000 to 30,000 B.C., or even before) Paleo-Siberians arrive in North America from Asia across Beringia (Bering Strait Land Bridge) and disperse throughout the Americas.

c. 15,000 (or much earlier)-8,000 B.C. Lithic (or Paleo-Indian) period, characterized by nomadic big-game hunting of now-extinct mammals, use of flaked stone tools, and invention of atlatl (spear-thrower).

    c. 10,000 B.C. (or earlier) Sandia Culture. Localized in Southwest; named after cave site in Sandia Mountains of New Mexico. Sandia points are about two to four inches long with a bulge on one side where attached to wooden shafts.

    c. 10,000 B.C. (or earlier)-8,000 B.C. Clovis (or Llano) Culture. Named after site in New Mexico, but Clovis points found throughout Americas, typically with mammoth and mastodon bones. Points are one and a half to five inches long, leaf-shaped, with fluting, i.e. grooves, along base on both sides.

    c. 9,500 (or earlier)-7,000 B.C. Folsom Culture. Named after site in New Mexico, but evidence of Folsom hunters found in much of North America, especially on Great Plains along with remains of bighorn bison. Folsom points have fluting on both sides extending almost entire length.

    c. 8,000–6,000 B.C. Plano Culture (or Plainview Culture after Plainview site in Texas). Associated with Great Plains and bighorn bison, based on findings of leaf-shaped points. More varied than cultures before them. Considered a transitional culture between Paleo-Indians and Archaic Indians.

c. 10,000–5,000 B.C. Pleistocene period (Ice Age) ends with retreat of glaciers and change of climate.

    c. 9,000–5,000 B.C. Big-game species become extinct.

    c. 8,000 B.C. Warm enough for cone-bearing trees.

    c. 6,000 B.C. Warm enough for broad-leaf trees.

c. 8,000–1,000 B.C. Archaic (or Foraging) period, characterized by nomadic hunting-gathering of varied fauna and flora, use of wide assortment of tools, and increasing ceremonialism.

    c. 9,000–5000 B.C. Old Cordilleran (or Cascade) Culture in Pacific Northwest along Columbia River. Cascade points are shaped like willow leaf; probably used to hunt small game. (Early stage represents protoarchaic forerunner of Archaic period.)

    c. 9,000–1,000 B.C. Desert Culture in Great Basin. First example of basketry in North America: woven containers from about 7,500 B.C. found at Danger Cave in Utah. (Early stage represents protoarchaic forerunner of Archaic period.)

    c. 7,000–500 B.C. Cochise Culture in Southwest. Probably offshoot of earlier Desert Culture. First evidence of agriculture north of Mexico: dried-up corn cobs of a cultivated species, dating from about 3,500 B.C., found at Bat Cave, New Mexico. Culture named after 19th-century Apache chief.

    c. 4,000–1,500 B.C. Old Copper Culture in western Great Lakes region. Name based on copper artifacts discovered among remains, earliest known use of metal among Indians north of Mexico.

    c. 3,000–1,000 B.C. Aleuts and Inuits migrate from Siberia to North America.

    c. 3,000–500 B.C. Red Paint People in present-day New England and eastern Canada. Name based on use of ground-up red iron ore to line graves.

c. 7,000–2,000 B.C. Beginnings of agriculture and pottery in Mesoamerica and North America.

    c. 7,000–5,000 B.C. Wild plants, including corn, gathered. Beginnings of cultivation in Mesoamerica.

    c. 5,000–3500 B.C. Cultivated strain of corn introduced in Mesoamerica.

    c. 4,500 B.C. Pottery introduced in Mesoamerica.

    c. 3,500 B.C. Cultivated corn as far north as New Mexico among Cochise Culture.

    c. 2,500 B.C. Improved hybrid strain of corn introduced.

    c. 2,500–1,500 B.C. Permanent villages established in Mesoamerica with agriculture-based economy. Irrigation developed.

    c. 2,000–1,500 B.C. Pottery made by Southwest Indians. Pottery-making spreads throughout North America.

c. 1,500 B.C.–A.D. 300 Preclassic period in Mesoamerica, characterized by growth of religious and economic centers with class system of royalty, priests, bureaucrats, merchants, craftsmen, and soldiers. Olmecs flourish on Gulf Coast east of present-day Mexico City, creating "mother civilization" of Mesoamerica, which influences other cultures to follow. Early Maya civilization in present-day Guatemala and Belize takes shape.

    c. 1,200 to 900 B.C. Olmec center of San Lorenzo dominant.

    c. 800 to 400 B.C. La Venta dominant.

    c. 100 B.C. to A.D. 300 Tres Zapotes dominant.

c. 1,000 B.C.–A.D. 1000 (or 1500) Formative period in North America, characterized by village life, agriculture, pottery, weaving, stone carving, ceremonial structures, and trade.

    c. 700 B.C.–A.D. 400 Adena Culture of moundbuilders in and around Ohio Valley. Burial mounds, plus effigy mounds with geometric and symbolic shapes; the Great Serpent Mound near present-day Peebles, Ohio, an effigy mound. Culture named after estate near present-day Chillicothe, Ohio.

    c. 300 B.C.–A.D. 1400 Mogollon Culture in Southwest, centered in Mogollon mountains. Mogollon Indians, perhaps descendants of Cochise peoples, considered first Southwest people to adopt farming, house-building, and pottery on wide scale. Mimbres subgroup produces black-on-white pottery from about A.D. 900 to A.D. 1300. Mogollon Indians probably ancestral to Zunis.

c. 100 B.C.–A.D. 700 Hopewell Culture of moundbuilders; centered along Ohio Valley, but Hopewell burial mounds, effigy mounds, and artifacts found over a much wider area of Midwest and East. Hopewell Indians probably ancestral to later eastern tribes.

c. 100 B.C.–A.D. 1300 Anasazi Culture in Southwest (100 B.C.–A.D. 700, Basket Maker period; A.D. 700–1300, Pueblo period.) Lived in pueblos and cliff-dwellings. Probably ancestral to contemporary Pueblo Indians. Culture name means "ancient ones" in Athapascan.

c. 100 B.C.–A.D. 1450 Hohokam Culture in Southwest, along Gila and Salt river valleys in present-day southern Arizona. Use of irrigation. Center at Snaketown (near present-day Phoenix) with about 100 pithouses. Acid-etching developed c. 1000. Probably ancestral to Pimas and Papagos. Culture name means "vanished ones" in Pima dialect of Uto-Aztecan.

c. A.D. 700–1500 Mississippian Culture (Temple Moundbuilders) in Mississippi Valley, with related Mississippian sites extending throughout much of Southeast and East. Cahokia in present-day Illinois, largest Mississippian population center, covering about 4,000 acres, with more than 100 temple, burial, and effigy mounds. Ancestral to Southeast Indians. From about 1000–1500, religion known as Southern Death Cult practiced.

c. A.D. 1000–1500 Ancestral Apaches and Navajos break off from northern Athapascans of western Canada and settle in Southwest.

c. A.D. 1200–1300 Native peoples abandon Great Plains, probably because of drought.

c. A.D. 1275 Abandonment of pueblos in Southwest, possibly because of drought or raiding Athapascans.

c. A.D. 1300–1400 Tribes begin migrating to Great Plains.

c. A.D. 300–900 Classic period in Mesoamerica, characterized by highly developed agricultural techniques, complex societies, city-states, massive stone architecture (including pyramids), pictograph writing systems, and calendars.

c. A.D. 300–700 City of Teotihuacan flourishes in Valley of Mexico, first true city of Mesoamerica with plazas, boulevards, parks, canals, drain conduits, marketplaces, workshops, apartment houses, and temple pyramids. Influence reaches over much of Mesoamerica as far as present-day Guatemala. (City's ruins later become known to Aztecs as "place of the gods.")

c. A.D. 300–900 Maya (Lowland Maya) civilization dominant in present-day Guatemala, east-central Mexico, and Belize. City-states at Bonampak, Copan, Palenque, Tikal, Uxmal, and other sites.

c. A.D. 700–900 Zapotecs flourish in Oaxaca with religious center at Mitla and city at Monte Alban.

c. A.D. 500–1000 Use of bow and arrow spreads throughout North America, gradually replacing atlatl, and spreading to Mesoamerica.

c. A.D. 900–1500 Postclassic period in Mesoamerica, drawing on earlier cultures with development of new techniques of agriculture and crafts.

c. A.D. 900–1200 Toltecs invade from north and become dominant in Valley of Mexico, founding city of Tula in 987. At its peak, Toltec Empire stretches from Gulf of Mexico to Pacific Ocean. A branch of Toltecs invade Yucatan Peninsula, interbreeding with Mayas and bringing about renaissance. Tula destroyed in 1160.

c. A.D. 900–1200 Maya civilization flourishes in highlands of present-day southern Guatemala, with city-states at Chama, Utatlan, and Kaminaljuya. Another strain of Maya culture in combination with invading Toltecs flourishes in northern Yucatan Peninsula after 1000, with population centers at Chichen Itza, Mayapam, and Tulum.

c. A.D. 900–1300 Mixtecs invade Zapotec territory, spreading southward from north into Valley of Oaxaca, overrunning cities of Mitla and Monte Alban.

c. A.D. 1000 Mesoamerican Indians begin using *cire perdue* (lost wax) process to cast copper bells, as metallurgy spreads northward from South America.

c. A.D. 1200–1500 Aztec civilization dominant. In 1325, Nahuatl-speaking Aztecs (Mexicas) build Tenochtitlan at site of Mexico City. Through conquest of area tribes, Aztec Empire eventually comprises five million people.

c. A.D. 985–1014 Vikings (Norsemen), including Leif Ericsson, Thorvald Ericsson, and Freydis, found settlements in North America and encounter *skraelings*, probably Inuits (Eskimos), or possibly Beothuks or Micmacs.

BIOGRAPHICAL DICTIONARY

(Native Americans mentioned in the timelines)

BEAR HUNTER (Wirasuap, "bear spirit"). (d. 1863). *Shoshone.* Bear Hunter was chief of a village on the Bear River, north of Great Salt Lake, in Utah. Indian raids in the Great Basin, sometimes referred to as the Shoshone Uprising, led to the Bear River Campaign of 1863 under Colonel Patrick E. Connor during which Bear Hunter was killed.

BIG BEAR (Mistahimaskwa). (1825–1888). *Plains Cree.* Big Bear led his band in support of the Metis in Canada's Second Riel Rebellion of 1885, participating in action at Frog Lake, Frenchman's Butte, and Loon Lake. After his surrender, he was imprisoned for almost three years along with fellow Cree chief Poundmaker, and died soon after his release.

BIG FOOT (Si Tanka; Spotted Elk). (c. 1825–1890). *Miniconjou Sioux.* After the War for the Black Hills of 1876–77, Big Foot's band was settled on the Cheyenne River Reservation in South Dakota. In 1890, during the Ghost Dance movement, on learning that Sitting Bull had been killed, Big Foot led his people toward the Pine Ridge Reservation to seek the protection of Red Cloud. His people were intercepted and eventually attacked at Wounded Knee Creek, where Big Foot was killed.

BLACK ELK (Hehaka Sapa). (1863–1950). *Oglala Sioux.* As a youth of 13, Black Elk participated in the Battle of Little Bighorn. As an adult, he lived on the Pine Ridge Reservation in South Dakota, where tribal members consulted with him for his visions. In 1886–89, he toured the eastern United States and Europe with Buffalo Bill Cody's Wild West Show. In 1890, he became involved with the Ghost Dance movement. In 1930–31, Nebraska poet John G. Neihardt interviewed Black Elk and recorded his oral history, published in 1932 as *Black Elk Speaks: The Life Story of a Holy Man of the Oglala Sioux.*

BLACK HAWK (Makataimeshekiakiak, Black Sparrow Hawk). (1767–1838). *Sac.* As leader of Sac and Fox militants, Black Hawk was willing to fight to keep tribal lands in Illinois in the Black Hawk War of 1832. White Cloud (Winnebago Prophet) of the Winnebagos was his ally; Keokuk, his rival. In 1833, as a prisoner of war, Black Hawk was taken to Washington, D.C., to meet President Andrew Jackson and tour eastern cities. Stripped of his homeland and his authority, he died in Iowa.

BLACK KETTLE (Moketavato). (c. 1803–1868). *Southern Cheyenne.* During the wars for the Southern Plains in the 1860s, Black Kettle advocated peace with whites. Yet his Southern Cheyenne band was attacked at Sand Creek in Colorado in 1865, and at Washita in the Indian Territory in 1868, where he was killed by troops under Lieutenant Colonel George Armstrong Custer.

BOWLEGS, BILLY (Holatamico, "alligator chief"). (c. 1810–1864). *Seminole.* In the Second Seminole War of 1835–42, Billy Bowlegs fought in many of the battles along with Osceola and other leaders. He carried on resistance in the Third Seminole War of 1855–58, which began when surveyors stole Seminole crops in the Great Cypress Swamp of Florida's Everglades. Following negotiations, Bowlegs took his band to lands on the north and south forks of the Canadian River in the Indian Territory. In 1861, he fought for the Union in the Civil War.

BRANT, JOSEPH (Joseph Brandt; Thayendanegea, "he places two bets"). (1742–1807). *Mohawk.* Joseph Brant grew up in the Mohawk Valley of New York. William Johnson, the land speculator and trader, married his sister Molly Brant. Brant acted as interpreter for Johnson, and personal secretary for Johnson's nephew Guy Johnson, with whom he traveled to England. Brant joined the Loyalist cause in the American Revolution, leading many raids on frontier settlements in New York and Pennsylvania. After the war, Brant settled in Ontario.

BUFFALO HORN. (d. 1878). *Bannock.* Although Buffalo Horn advocated peace with whites, he agreed to lead his warriors in battle because of settlers' violation of Bannock treaty rights. The first clash of the Bannock War came in June 1878 in southern Idaho between Indians and a volunteer patrol from Silver City; Buffalo Horn was killed. His warriors headed westward into Oregon and regrouped at Steens Mountain with Northern Paiutes from the Malheur Reservation. The Paiute chief Egan then assumed command of the combined force; on Egan's death, the Paiute medicine man Oytes led the uprising.

CHITTO HARJO (Crazy Snake; Wilson Jones). (1846–1912). *Creek.* A tribal traditionalist in the Indian Territory, Chitto Harjo opposed the General Allotment Act of 1887. With other northern Creeks, who called themselves Snakes, he created the alternative Snake Government in 1897, and carried out acts of civil disobedience, one of them known as the Crazy Snake (or Snake) Uprising of 1901.

COCHISE ("hardwood"). (c. 1812–1874). *Chiricahua Apache.* Cochise, son-in-law of Mimbreno chief Mangas Coloradas, was active in the Apache Wars of the 1870s, conducting raids from the Dragoon Mountains of southern Arizona. In 1872, he agreed to stop his band's raids in exchange for a Chiricahua Reservation at Apache Pass, maintaining peace until his death. His elder son Taza, who succeeded him as chief, attempted to maintain the peace agreement. On Taza's death, Cochise's younger son Naiche joined forces with Geronimo, and the reservation was dissolved in 1876.

CORNPLANTER (Gyantwaia; John O'Bail). (c. 1735–1836). *Seneca.* Cornplanter, half-brother of Handsome Lake, was a war chief who sided with the French in the French and Indian War of 1753–1763. In the American Revolution, however, he sided with the British. After the war, he took part in numerous treaty negotiations, helping his tribe keep some of their homelands in western New York. Cornplanter's influence among his people led them to support the Americans in the War of 1812.

CORNSTALK (Wynepuechsika). (c. 1720–1777). *Shawnee.* Cornstalk, principal chief of the Ohio Shawnees and ally of the

French in the French and Indian War, threw his support behind Pontiac in his rebellion against the British in 1763. Well-known as a strategist and orator, he was the most influential leader in Lord Dunmore's War of 1774. In 1777, during the American Revolution, because of continuing Shawnee raids, Cornstalk was taken hostage along with his son, and killed by militiamen who stormed the jail.

CRAZY HORSE (Tashunka Witco). (c. 1842–1877). *Oglala-Brule Sioux*. Crazy Horse fought in the War for the Bozeman Trail of 1866–68 under the Oglala chief Red Cloud. He became a war chief of the Oglalas, with some Brule followers as well; through marriage to a Cheyenne woman, he also had followers among the Northern Cheyennes. Crazy Horse fought in many engagements of the War for the Black Hills of 1876–77. He eventually surrendered with some 800 followers at the Red Cloud Agency in northwestern Nebraska on May 5, 1877, where he was killed in a fight with Indian police.

CROW DOG (Kangi Sunka). (c. 1835–c. 1910). *Brule Sioux*. In 1881, in a dispute with Spotted Tail, leader of the Rosebud Reservation in South Dakota, Crow Dog shot and killed him. In 1883, the Supreme Court pardoned Crow Dog in the case of Ex Parte Crow Dog, ruling that the federal courts had no jurisdiction over crimes committed on reservation treaty lands. In 1885, Congress passed the Major Crimes Act, providing that an Indian committing a major crime against a fellow Indian, such as murder or burglary, was subject to the laws of the territory or state where the crime was committed. Crow Dog later became a proponent of the Ghost Dance.

CURTIS, CHARLES. (1860–1936). *Kaw-Osage*. Charles Curtis's Osage ancestors were adopted members of the Kaw (Kansa) tribe, and he attended an Indian mission school on the Kaw Reservation, then a high school in Topeka, Kansas. In 1881, Curtis was admitted to the bar and soon entered politics as a Republican. He was elected to the House of Representatives, serving eight terms in 1892–1907. He was later elected to the Senate, serving in 1907–13 and 1915–29. Following an unsuccessful bid for the presidential nomination, he ran with Herbert Hoover in 1928, serving as vice president in 1929–33.

DELAWARE PROPHET (Neolin, "enlightened one"). (fl. 1760s). *Lenni Lenape*. About 1760, Delaware Prophet had a religious experience in which he claimed he journeyed to the Spirit World, encountered the Master of Life, and received a set of laws concerning a return to traditional ways. He began preaching among the Lenni Lenapes (Delaware) Indians of the Muskingum Valley of Ohio and among other tribes in the Old Northwest. His message helped Pontiac achieve unity among the region's tribes.

DELGADITO (Herrero Delgadito, "slender little metal worker"). (c. 1830–c. 1870). *Navajo*. Medicine man Delgadito participated with his brother Barboncito and their followers in the Navajo War of 1863–66. He was among the first Navajos to be taken to Bosque Redondo in eastern New Mexico in early 1864. He later signed the treaty of 1868, allowing the Navajos to return to their ancestral lands in Arizona. He was known for his silverwork and taught his people the craft.

DELSHAY. (c. 1835–1874). *Tonto Apache*. In 1868, Delshay's Tonto band of Western Apaches lived near Camp McDowell on the Verde River in Arizona. In 1871, he requested that they be allowed to live in the Sunflower Valley, closer to their ancestral homeland. In 1872, in response to a public outcry about continuing Western Apache raids, General George Crook launched the Tonto Basin Campaign and put a price on Delshay's head; he is believed to have been killed by a fellow Apache.

DONNACONNA (Donacona). (d. c. 1539). *Huron*. In 1534, at Gaspe Harbor in Quebec, Donnaconna met Jacques Cartier's first expedition. After negotiations and an exchange of gifts, he allowed his two sons to travel with Cartier, who took them to France. In 1535, on the St. Lawrence River near the Huron village of Stadacona (present-day Quebec City), Donnaconna and his men met the returning Cartier and his sons. In 1536, Donnaconna traveled back to France with Cartier, and was presented to King Francis I. He contracted a European disease and died abroad.

DORION, MARIE (Dorion Woman; Marie of the Iowas). (1786–c.1853). *Iowa*. At age 20, Marie Dorion met and married Pierre Dorion, Jr., in Arkansas, a mixed French Canadian and Yankton Sioux trader in the employ of Manuel Lisa. During a trip to St. Louis, Pierre Dorion left Lisa's outfit to join the expedition backed by John Jacob Astor and headed by Wilson Price Hunt. Marie Dorion acted as a guide and interpreter for the Astorians, who departed St. Louis in March 1811 and reached Astoria at the mouth of the Columbia River in Oregon in February 1812. She spent the rest of her life in the Far West.

DRAGGING CANOE (Tsiyu-Gunsini). (c. 1730–1792). *Cherokee*. Dragging Canoe, son of peace chief Attakullakulla, led a dissident group of Chickimauga Cherokees who refused to sign the Treaty of Sycamore Shoals in 1775. During the subsequent fighting in the American Revolution, Dragging Canoe accepted arms from the British and attacked trans-Appalachian settlements, along with Creek allies under Alexander McGillivray. Militias were raised for a campaign of destruction of Cherokee villages and crops until a tenuous peace was established.

DULL KNIFE (Tahmelapashme). (c. 1810–1883). *Northern Cheyenne*. Dull Knife was active in the Cheyenne-Arapaho War in Colorado in 1864–65, as well as Red Cloud's War for the Bozeman Trail of 1866–68. He was one of the signers of the Treaty of Fort Laramie in 1868. He also joined the Sioux in the War for the Black Hills of 1876–77. In 1876, Colonel Ranald Mackenzie's Fourth Cavalry attacked Dull Knife's camp on the Red Fork of the Powder River in Wyoming. Upon surrender, Dull Knife and his followers were sent to the Indian Territory. In September 1878, nearly 300 men, women, and children, led by Dull Knife and Little Wolf, set out northward for their ancestral homeland, but were eventually captured and held at army agencies. Dull Knife died the year before the Northern Cheyennes were granted the Tongue River Reservation in Montana.

ESKIMINZIN (Eskaminzin, "angry men standing in line for him"). (c. 1825–1890). *Aravaipa-Pinal Apache*. In 1871, with increasing tensions between Apaches and whites, Eskiminzin led his peaceful Aravaipa band of Western Apaches to Camp Grant, Arizona. But citizens of Tucson blamed his band for raids; in April, a vigilante force slaughtered as many as 150 of his followers, mostly women and children. In a subsequent trial, the leaders of the attack were acquitted. Eskiminzin, despite his neutral stance, was later arrested and sent to Florida with Geronimo's Chiricahuas, then to Alabama. In 1889, he was finally allowed to return home, dying the next year.

GALL (Pizi). (1840–1894). *Hunkpapa Sioux*. Gall, the adopted younger brother of Sitting Bull, along with other young warriors such as Crazy Horse, devised decoy techniques in Red Cloud's War for the Bozeman Trail of 1866–68, luring soldiers and emigrants into traps. In the War for the Black Hills of 1876–77, he acted as Sitting Bull's principal strategist. He played a key role in the Indian victory at Little Bighorn in 1876. After the war, he fled to Canada with Sitting Bull, eventually settling at the Standing Rock Reservation in North Dakota.

GARRA, ANTONIO. (d. 1852). *Cupeno*. During the California Gold Rush, Antonio Garra, a medicine man and chief of a band along the San Luis Rey River in southern California, tried to lead a general revolt of the region's tribes against white settlers. Juan Antonio, a Cahuilla, threw his support to the whites and captured his rival Garra in late 1851. After a court martial by the state militia, Garra was executed.

GERONIMO (Goyathlay, "one who yawns"). (c.1825–1909). *Chiricahua Apache*. As a young man, Geronimo fought under Cochise and Mangas Coloradas. He was not a hereditary chief, but gained prestige through deeds. He also came to be considered a medicine man by his people. In the 1880s, Geronimo became the principal war chief of the Apache militants; warriors such as Chato, Juh, Loco, Naiche, Nana fought alongside him. In 1886, after time on and off the San Carlos Reservation in Arizona, Geronimo surrendered for the last time at Skeleton Canyon, about 65 miles south of the Apache Pass. Apache prisoners were sent by rail to Fort Pickens and Fort Marion in Florida, then to Mount Vernon Barracks in Alabama. In 1894, the last of the prisoners were allowed to resettle at Fort Sill among Comanches and Kiowas. In his new home, Geronimo took up farming, dictated his memoirs, and made public appearances. He was never granted permission to return to his homeland before his death from pneumonia.

GREAT SUN (Grand Soleil). (d. c. 1730). *Natchez*. "Great Sun" was a hereditary title of the Natchez, bestowed upon the principal chief. The Great Sun recorded in history ruled during the early 1700s, when the French began settling along the lower Mississippi River. In 1716, the French built Fort Rosalie on choice Natchez land in Mississippi. The Great Sun led the Natchez Revolt of 1729 against the French, retaking ancestral homelands. But an army of French soldiers and Choctaw warriors recaptured Fort Rosalie. The Great Sun managed to escape up the Red River, where the French attacked them a year later and forced a surrender. It is thought that he was taken to New Orleans and executed.

GUANCANAGARI. (fl. 1490s). *Arawak*. Guancanagari, one of five chieftains who ruled Hispaniola (Haiti and Dominican Republic), provided aid when Christopher Columbus's ship *Santa Maria* was wrecked. After Columbus's departure, the cacique tried to prevent an attack on the Spanish garrison at Navidad. Wounded in battle, he retreated into the mountains. With Columbus's large-scale colonizing expedition of 1493–94, Guancanagari again allied himself with the Spanish against militant Arawaks. Suffering defeat, he spent the rest of his life in the mountains in exile from his people.

HANCOCK (King Hancock). (fl. early 1700s). *Tuscarora*. Because of expanding white settlement, the Tuscarora chief Hancock led his warriors in raids against settlements between Pamlico Sound and the Neuse River in North Carolina. In 1712, the colonies of North and South Carolina sent soldiers in an invasion of Tuscarora territory. Tuscarora survivors fled northward to New York and settled among the five tribes of the Iroquois League.

HANDSOME LAKE (Skaniadariio, "beautiful lake"). (1749–1815). *Seneca*. In 1799, Handsome Lake, the half-brother of Cornplanter, alcoholic and sick, experienced a series of visions in which he claimed he was taken on a spiritual journey by four messengers. Afterward, he stopped drinking and regained his health. He preached the rejection of many white customs, especially the use of alcohol, advocating self-purification through traditional beliefs. His message became organized as the Code of Handsome Lake, sometimes called the Longhouse Religion.

HUNT, GEORGE (Hau). (1854–1933). *Kwakiutl-Tlingit*. George Hunt was the son of a Tlingit woman and an English administrator of the Hudson Bay Company's. Although Hunt's mother was Tlingit, he was raised among the Kwakiutls of British Columbia and married a Kwakiutl woman. In the 1880s, he worked as a guide, interpreter, and informant for scientific projects. In 1903, Hunt helped organize the Northwest Coast Indian exhibit of the American Museum of Natural History in New York. He was eventually selected as a chief of the Kwakiutls.

INKPADUTA ("scarlet point"). (c. 1815–c. 1882). *Wahpekute Sioux*. In 1828, after his father had killed the principal chief of their tribe, Inkpaduta's family became outcasts among the Wahpekutes and other Santee Sioux bands. In 1848, on the death of his father, Inkpaduta became chief of the small band. Inkpaduta led the Spirit Lake Uprising of 1855 against settlers in northwest Iowa, and participated in the Minnesota Uprising of 1862–63. He migrated further westward in later years and reportedly fought at Little Bighorn, after which he fled to Canada.

ISHI ("man"). (c. 1862–1916). *Yahi (Yana)*. In 1865–68, miners launched attacks on a Yahi village on Mill Creek in northeastern California. Only a dozen or so Yahis escaped into the wilderness, one of them a boy about six years old. Over the next decades, the surviving Yahis hid out from whites and lived off the land, occasionally pilfering food from mining camps and ranchers. By 1908, only one Yahi remained; he lived in the wilderness three more years. Finally, half-starving, he walked to the town of Oroville. The Anthropological Museum of the University of California in San Francisco took full responsibility for Ishi. He worked as an informant for anthropologists Alfred Kroeber, Theodora Kroeber, and Thomas Waterman, as well as a groundskeeper at the museum, eventually dying of tuberculosis.

JOHN (Old John). (fl. 1850s). *Rogue River*. With miners and settlers expropriating Indian lands, Old John, chief of the Takelma and Tututni Indians living along the Rogue River Valley in southwestern Oregon, armed his followers by having them prospect gold and trade it for guns and ammunition. A cycle of raids and counterraids erupted in the early 1850s until troops defeated the militants in the Rogue River War of 1855–56. Most of John's followers were relocated to the Siletz Reservation to the north. Old John and his son Adam were sent to Alcatraz in San Francisco Bay. By the time they returned to their homeland, few remembered them.

JOSEPH (Chief Joseph, Young Joseph; Heinmot Tooyalaket, "thunder coming from water over land"). (c. 1840–1904). *Nez Perce*. On the death of Old Joseph (Tuekakas) in 1871, leadership of his band in Oregon's Wallowa Valley passed to Young Joseph and his brother Ollikut. Like their father, they passively resisted relocation to the Nez Perce Reservation near Fort Lapwai, Idaho. Continuing white settlement on Indian lands led to the unrest in the Nez Perce War of 1877, also known as the Flight of the Nez Perces, consisting of a 1,700-mile journey to Montana, just short of the Canadian border. Survivors were taken to Fort Leavenworth, Kansas, then to the Indian Territory. In 1885, Chief Joseph was sent to the Colville Reservation in Washington, where he lived out his life.

KAMIAKIN ("he will not go"). (c. 1800–1877). *Yakima*. Kamiakin was the son of a Yakima woman, but was related to the Nez Perces, Palouses, and Spokanes through his father. Because of his ancestry and marital relationships, and by force of his personality, he had influence among many Washington and Oregon tribes. Cayuse, Wallawalla, Umatilla, and Sinkiuse warriors all participated in the Yakima War of 1855–56. Then, in 1858, he led Yakimas and warriors of other tribes—Coeur d'Alene, Spokane, and Palouse—in the Coeur d'Alene War (or Spokane War). After defeat, Kamiakin managed to escape into British Columbia where he hid out among the Kootenays. He returned in 1861 and lived out his life in peace on the Spokane Reservation.

KATLIAN (Kotlian). (fl. early 1800s). *Tlingit*. Russian fur traders reached Tlingit lands along the the Alexander Archipelago and southern Alaskan coast in the 1790s, establishing a post at Sitka on Baranov Island in 1799. In 1802, Katlian, principal chief of the Sitka band, led an attack on Sitka, capturing it and taking back the pelts hunted on Tlingit lands. Katlian's warriors held the post for two years until Baranov returned with an armada of ships and a force of 120 Russians and nearly 1,000 Aleuts.

KENNEKUK ("putting his foot down"; Kickapoo Prophet). (c. 1785–1852). *Kickapoo*. Kennekuk, a shaman and chief of a band living along the Osage River in Illinois, preached abstention from liquor and criminal behavior, as well as the use of meditation, fasting, and wooden prayer sticks in order to achieve a new tribal paradise. With pressure to have his band relocate to Missouri, Kennekuk used passive resistance. Meeting frequently with officials, he expressed a willingness to depart westward, while giving excuses for delays, such as the harvest, illness, or evil omens. His band finally moved in 1833.

KICKING BIRD (Tene-angpote). (1835–1875). *Kiowa*. Kicking Bird was one of the signers of the Little Arkansas Treaties of 1865, and the Treaty of Medicine Lodge of 1867. He also headed the peace faction in the Indian territory during the Red River War of 1874–75. After the war, he was assigned the difficult task of deciding which of the militants would be sent to exile at Fort Marion, Florida. Less than a week later, Kicking Bird died, probably from poison. Legend has it that the militant shaman Mamanti (Sky Walker) used his magical powers to will Kicking Bird dead.

KINTPUASH (Captain Jack). (c. 1840–1873). *Modoc*. In 1864, the Modocs were coerced into signing away their lands and relocating to the Klamath Reservation in southern Oregon. A faction under Kintpuash, nicknamed Captain Jack by whites, attempted to maintain a home on Modoc lands in northern California. In 1872, the federal government sent troops to force them back to Oregon, starting the Modoc War. The freedom fighters made a stand at the Lava Beds from January until June of 1873. Kintpuash was convicted and hanged with three other Modocs for the killing of General Edward Canby and peace commissioner Eleasar Thomas at a peace council.

LITTLE CROW (Cetan Wakan Mani). (c. 1810–1863). *Mdewakanton Sioux*. In 1834, on his father's death, Little Crow assumed leadership of the Santee band at the site of present-day South St. Paul, Minnesota. In 1862, when the Indian agent refused to distribute stockpiled food to the Santee Sioux because he wanted kickbacks, Little Crow led an uprising known as the Minnesota Uprising. In May 1863, after defeat, Little Crow sought British help at Fort Garry (Winnipeg, Manitoba), but was turned away. The following July, near the town of Hutchinson, Minnesota, while picking berries with his 16-year-old son Wowinapa, Little Crow was attacked and killed by settlers who sought the 25-dollar bounty on Sioux scalps.

LITTLE TURTLE (Michikinikwa). (1752–1812). *Miami-Mahican*. In the American Revolution, Little Turtle supported the Loyalists. Following American victory in 1783, more and more settlers began squatting on Indian lands. Little Turtle became principal war chief of the allied tribes in their resistance against encroachments. His strategy of concealment and swift small strikes to confuse the enemy led to victories against generals Arthur St. Clair and Josiah Harmar in 1790–91. With a larger army mustered under "Mad" Anthony Wayne, Little Turtle counseled peace, but his advice was ignored. He gave up his command to the Shawnee Blue Jacket and led only a small party of Miamis in battle at Fallen Timbers, a defeat for the alliance. Little Turtle was one of the signers of the Treaty of Fort Greenville in 1795, in which tribal representatives were forced to sign away more than half of Ohio.

LOWRY, HENRY BERRY (Lowrie, Lowery). (c. 1856–c. 1872). *Lumbee*. The Lumbees of Robeson County, North Carolina, were ill-treated during the Civil War and forced to participate under poor conditions. In 1864, Henry Berry Lowry, a teenager at the time, established a small guerilla band made up of Lumbees, blacks, and at least one white, who raided plantations and distributed their booty to the region's poor. They fought the Home Guard in numerous skirmishes, as well as the Ku Klux Klan. Their raids continued after the Civil War during which time they fought federal troops. Berry was captured and escaped three times, contributing to his growing legendary status. In 1872, he disappeared and is thought to have been killed. But the bounty on his head was never collected. As late as the 1930s, some claimed he still lived.

MALACA. (d. 1817). *Patwin*. In 1817, the Spanish governor of Alta California instructed the commander of San Francisco Presidio to pacify the Patwins to the north. A force under Don Jose Sanchez defeated Malaca's warriors in battle. The Indians retreated to the village of Suisun. When the Spanish advanced on them, the chief and the majority of his people chose to burn themselves to death rather than live out their lives in slavery. Others escaped to the neighboring village of Chief Motti on the west bank of the Sacramento River.

MANGAS COLORADAS (Mangus Colorado). (c. 1797–1863). *Mimbreno Apache*. Mangas Coloradas was the leader of the Mimbreno Apaches, inhabiting the Mimbres Mountains of southwestern New Mexico. His band resisted non-Indian expansion in the region in the 1830s-50s. In the early 1860s, during the Civil War, when federal troops were called back East, a column under Colonel James Carleton out of California headed into the Southwest. In 1862, Mangas's Mimbrenos and his son-in-law Cochise's Chiricahuas attacked Carleton's advance company at

Apache Pass. Mangas took a bullet in the chest. His warriors carried him to Mexico, where he recovered. The next year, he was tricked into coming to a council by officials, taken captive, then murdered by his guards.

MANUELITO. (c. 1818–1894). *Navajo.* Manuelito served as war chief during the Navajo War of 1863–66 in Arizona and New Mexico, leading raids and defending against General James Carleton's troops led by Christopher "Kit" Carson in the field. He held out longer than the other headmen, surrendering in September 1866. He was sent to Bosque Redondo in eastern New Mexico and was one of the delegation of chiefs who traveled to Washington to plead their case for a return to their homeland. Finally, in 1868, the federal government granted the Navajos reservation lands in their Chuska Mountain homeland. Manuelito served as principal chief from 1870 to 1884.

MAQUINNA. (fl. early 1800s). *Nootka.* Maquinna was chief of the Mooachaht band living on the Nootka Sound of Vancouver Island. In 1803, he led warriors in an attack on the trading ship *Boston* from the port of that name. The Indians killed the entire crew except the blacksmith John Jewitt and the sailmaker Thompson. Maquinna kept them prisoners among his people for two years until they were liberated by the crew of the *Lydia*, also out of Boston. Jewitt wrote a captivity narrative about the incident.

MARIN. (fl. 1820s). *Pomo.* Marin was chief of the Gallinomero band of Pomo Indians in northern California. In 1815 or 1816, his warriors were defeated in battle by Spanish soldiers. Marin was captured and taken to San Francisco. On escaping, he launched more raids against the Spanish, keeping them out of Pomo territory. In 1824, after Mexican independence from Spain, Mexican troops moved on Marin and defeated him. Marin spent a year in jail, then lived out his life at the San Rafael Mission in his homeland.

MASSASOIT (Massassoit, "great chief"). (c. 1590–1661). *Wampanoag.* Massasoit was grand sachem of the Wampanoag Confederacy, ruling over bands from Narragansett Bay to Cape Cod. His main village was near present-day Bristol, Rhode Island. He was introduced to the Pilgrims at Plymouth in March 1621 by the Abenaki Indian Samoset. With the Wampanoag Indian Squanto acting as interpreter, Massasoit negotiated a treaty with the Pilgrims. Massasoit had his people teach the Pilgrims planting methods. That autumn, Massasoit came to Plymouth with 60 to 100 followers for the first Thanksgiving feast. Massasoit's son Metacom led the uprising known as King Philip's War of 1675–76.

MATONABBEE. (c. 1736-1782). *Chipewyan.* Matonabbee was born near Fort Prince of Wales at the mouth of the Churchill River on the west side of Hudson's Bay. His father died soon after he was born, and Richard Norton, Hudson's Bay Company governor at the fort, raised the boy. When Norton returned to England, Matonabbee's Chipewyan relatives took him into their hunting band, which roamed the Barren Grounds of northern Manitoba, northern Saskatchewan, and eastern Northwest Territories. At the age of 16, Matonabbee returned to Fort Prince of Wales and began working for the British as a hunter and negotiator among warring tribes. In 1770, Matonabbee, now a chief, offered to aid the Englishman Samuel Hearne in his efforts to locate the Northwest Passage and find a source of copper; Hearne's two previous attempts on a northern expedition had failed. Matonabbee suggested attaching Chipewyan families to the expedition to protect against hostile bands and help in hunting.

The Third Coppermine Expedition of 1771-72 reached the Coppermine River and followed it to the Arctic Ocean. Hearne learned that the river was not the hoped-for Northwest Passage. He found only surface samples of copper, not productive mines. Ten years later, after a smallpox epidemic had killed many of his people, Matonabbee committed suicide by hanging himself.

McGILLIVRAY, ALEXANDER (Hoboi-hili-miko, "good child king"). (1759–1793). *Creek.* Alexander McGillivray was born in the Creek village of Little Tallassie along the Coosa River in eastern Alabama. His father was a Scottish trader, his mother of Creek and French ancestry. In the American Revolution, because of Loyalist ties, McGillivray supported the English as a colonel, attacking American settlements in Georgia and eastern Tennessee. After the war, in 1784, McGillivray signed a military and trade agreement with the Spanish; he was known to them as "Emperor" of the Creek and Seminole Nations. With the growth of his trading empire, he increased his ties with U.S. interests as well.

McINTOSH, WILLIAM. (1775–1825). *Creek.* The son of a Scottish trader and Creek woman, William McIntosh took a pro-American stance. He supported the United States as a brigadier general in the War of 1812. He joined General Andrew Jackson in the Creek War of 1813–14 and the First Seminole War of 1817–18. Because of his signing away of Creek lands in the Treaty of Indian Springs in 1825, he was sentenced to death in tribal council by the militant faction. Menewa led the war party that carried out the execution.

METACOM (King Philip, Metacomet, Potacomet, "the far away place"). *Wampanoag.* (c. 1639–1676). Metacom's village was located on the west shore of Mount Hope Bay near present-day Bristol, Rhode Island. He and his brother Wamsutta (Alexander) attempted to maintain good relations with the colonists as their father Massasoit had done. His brother's mysterious death following an arrest by officials, and increasing violation of Indian legal and land rights, led Metacom, or King Philip, as he was known to the colonists, to plan a rebellion. Narragansets under Canonchet as well as Nipmuc warriors joined the cause. In 1675, small bands of warriors attacked outlying settlements throughout New England from the Connecticut River to the Atlantic Coast. The New England Confederation of Colonies mustered armies which attacked Indian villages, burning wigwams and destroying crops. The culminating battle was the Great Swamp Fight in December 1676, resulting in the destruction of the main Narraganset village. Metacom was tracked down and killed the following August.

MOMADAY, NATACHEE SCOTT. (1934–). *Kiowa-Cherokee.* N. Scott Momaday was born in Lawton, Oklahoma, and grew up on a reservation. A professor of English, he has become known for both his prose and poetry on the Native American experience, including *House Made of Dawn* (1968), the story of a modern Indian, and *The Way to Rainy Mountain* (1969), about Kiowa history and legend.

NAMPEYO (Snake Woman). (c. 1860–1942). *Hopi-Tewa.* Nampeyo of the Hano Pueblo in Arizona became interested in ancient pottery forms and designs. Her husband Lesou was employed by the archaeologist J. Walter Fewkes and helped Nampeyo find potsherds showing the old forms. Nampeyo developed her own style based on the traditional designs. Her influence led to a renaissance of pottery-making among her people and the elevation of pottery to an art form. Her four daughters also became well-known potters.

NUMAGA (Young Winnemucca). (d. 1871). *Northern Paiute*. Numaga was chief of a Northern Paiute band living near the Carson Valley in western Nevada. Like his uncle Winnemucca and cousin Sarah Winnemucca, Numaga counseled peace with whites. On May 7, 1860, following the abduction and rape of two Paiute girls by traders, a war party attacked and burned Williams Station, a Central Overland Mail and Pony Express station along the California Trail, north of Pyramid Lake. Settlers and miners in the region organized a force of volunteers under Major William Ormsby. With the approach of troops, Numaga agreed to lead his warriors in battle and set a trap at the Big Bend of the Truckee River Valley. His warriors hid behind sagebrush on both sides of the pass. As many as 46 whites died in the Indian attack on May 12. California volunteers were organized under former Texas Ranger John Coffee Hays. On June 3, the force skirmished with the Paiutes near the site of Ormsby's defeat, then pursued the Indians to Pinnacle Mountain, where Numaga's warriors were routed. That summer, the army established Fort Churchill in the region to keep the Carson Branch of the California Trail open, and Numaga negotiated a lasting peace with whites. He died of tuberculosis 11 years later.

OACPICAGIGUA, LUIS. (fl. 1750s). *Pima*. Luis Oacpicagigua served the Spanish as a captain-general. On witnessing the growth of mining in northern Mexico and southern Arizona and the resulting forced labor among the Indians, he plotted and organized a general uprising. Starting in November 1751, Pimas attacked a number of missions and rancherias. Spanish officials ordered presidio captains and their troops into the field and managed to subdue the rebels through both military action and negotiations. Don Luis negotiated his freedom by agreeing to supervise the rebuilding of destroyed churches.

OCONOSTOTA ("groundhog sausage"). (c. 1710–1785). *Cherokee*. Attakullakulla was the principal Cherokee peace chief, and Oconostota, the war chief. With support from the Creeks, Oconostota led a party of Cherokees in a siege of Fort Prince George, South Carolina, in 1760, the start of the Cherokee War. He also headed a successful siege of Fort Loudon in present-day Tennessee. The war lasted two years. It took two armies and the destruction of Indian villages and crops to defeat the insurgents. During the American Revolution, Oconostota sided with his old enemies, the English, against the Americans; he was joined in this effort by Dragging Canoe, son of Attakullakulla.

OPECHANCANOUGH. (1564–1646). *Powhatan (Pamunkey)*. On Chief Powhatan's death in 1618, Opechancanough became the leader of the Powhatan Confederacy. Because of the colonists' expanding tobacco fields, which ruined the Indians' hunting grounds, Opechancanough ordered a surprise attack in 1622. A colonial army defeated the Indians, but both sides continued their raids for 10 years. Finally, in 1632, they agreed on a peace treaty. Twelve years later, in 1644, when he was supposedly about 100 years old and had to be carried to battle on a litter, Opechancanough ordered another attack. In 1646, a force of militiamen captured Opechancanough and carried him on his litter back to Jamestown. He was jeered by an angry crowd and later shot by a guard.

ORATAMIN (Oratamy). (d. c. 1667). *Wappinger*. Oratamin was a chief of the Hackensack band, part of the Wappinger Confederacy, living on the Hudson River. In 1639, the Dutch governor-general of New Netherland, Willem Kieft, began a policy of extermination of Indians to make room for Dutch settlers. In February 1643, a number of Wappinger families fled to the Dutch settlement of Pavonia for protection from Mohawks hired by the Dutch. Dutch soldiers attacked the refugees while they slept, killing and beheading about 80, many of them women and children, and taking 30 prisoners. The soldiers brought the 80 heads back to New Amsterdam, where they played kickball with them. Following the Pavonia Massacre, Hudson River Indians from both the Wappinger and Lenni Lenape (Delaware) confederacies rose up in rebellion, raiding Dutch settlements. Trading and farming were disrupted throughout New Netherland as settlers fled to New Amsterdam on Manhattan Island. During this period, the Dutch built a defensive wall in lower Manhattan, where Wall Street is today. An army of Dutch and English soldiers under Captain John Underhill began a campaign of attacking bands of Indians and destroying villages and crops. Oratamin spoke on behalf of the Hackensacks, Manhattans, Tappans, and Sintsincks of the allied Wappinger and Lenni Lenape confederacies at a peace council in April 1643, but fighting soon erupted again. He participated in a second treaty at Fort Amsterdam on Manhattan Island in August 1645, and a third in July 1649. In 1655, another incident led to further violence. A Dutch farmer killed a Lenni Lenape woman for stealing peaches from his orchard, and Hudson River Indians again began raiding Dutch settlements and taking prisoners. The new governor-general, Peter Stuyvesant, ordered out a militia force which succeeded in freeing the hostages. The violence shifted up the Hudson, with raids and counterraids between the Dutch and the Esophus band. In 1660, Stuyvesant began a policy of holding Indian children as hostages in New Amsterdam to extort good behavior from the area tribes. The Esophus insurgents agreed to peace in May 1664. Oratamin helped negotiate the final agreement. That same year, English troops invaded and captured New Netherland, which became New York, ending the Dutch claim in North America. Oratamin was asked to help in negotiations in the next years, but was too weakened by age to participate.

OSCEOLA ("black drink crier"). (c. 1803–1838). *Seminole*. Osceola fought in the First Seminole War of 1817–1818 as a teenager. With the Indian Removal Act of 1830, the Seminoles of Florida were pressured into removal to the Indian Territory. Osceola traveled from band to band, urging his people to stay on their ancestral homelands. Seminole leaders took their families into the swamps, safe from military round-ups, then, starting in 1835, waged an effective guerilla campaign. When Osceola agreed to attend a peace council at Fort Augustine in 1837, General Thomas Jesup ordered his arrest despite a flag of truce. Osceola was imprisoned at Fort Moultrie near Charleston, South Carolina, where he died the next year. Despite the loss of the leading war chief and the destruction of their homes and possessions, the rebels held out for several more years. Many among them never agreed to the terms of removal.

OURAY. (c. 1820 or c. 1833–1880). *Ute-Apache*. Ouray's father was a Jicarilla Apache adopted into the Utes; his mother, a Tabeguache Ute. Ouray spent much of his youth working for Mexican sheepherders, later establishing his reputation among the Tabeguaches (later known as the Uncompahgres) of southwestern Colorado in warfare against the Sioux and Kiowas. Ouray learned Spanish and English in addition to several different Indian languages. With his father's death in 1860, he became chief of his band. He made several trips to Washington, D.C. Because of his diplomatic efforts during the Ute War of 1879, hostages were released unharmed and most Ute warriors were pardoned for their involvement.

PACOMIO. (fl. 1820s). *Chumash.* Pacomio was raised and educated by Spanish missionaries at La Purisima Mission in the Santa Barbara district of California, and became a skilled carpenter. Dissatisfied with the treatment of his people by the Spanish, he planned a general uprising of Mission Indians. In March 1824, he led about 2,000 Indians on La Purisima, capturing it and placing the soldiers in jail. The Indians at Santa Inez and Santa Barbara also rebelled. Yet, because of Spanish counterattacks and the failure of other Mission Indians to participate, Pacomio's rebellion came to a gradual end. He himself surrendered and was allowed to live in peace at Monterey.

PALMA, SALVADOR. (fl. 1780s). *Yuma (Quechan).* Salvador Palma was chief of the Yuman-speaking Quechans living along the Colorado River near the present Arizona-California border. In July 1781, he and his brother Ygnacio Palma led warriors in attacks on Spanish missions in the region, killing perhaps as many as 95 priests, soldiers, and settlers, and capturing 76 women and children. That year and the next, the Spanish launched unsuccessful expeditions against the rebels. The Quechans and other Yumans retained control of the Colorado River for years to come.

PARKER, ELY SAMUEL (Donehogawa, "he holds the door open"). (c. 1828–1895). *Seneca.* After an education at non-Indian schools, Ely Parker, the grandson of post-Revolutionary chief Red Jacket, worked as an interpreter, informant, and researcher for the scholar Lewis Henry Morgan, then studied and worked in civil engineering. In 1858–61, he was a superintendent of government works at Galena, Illinois, where he befriended Ulysses Grant, who, in May 1863, arranged for him a commission as captain of engineers. In August 1864, Grant assigned Parker as his military secretary. Parker was present at Lee's surrender at Appomattox. On his election to president in 1868, Grant appointed Parker his commissioner of Indian Affairs. Parker later lived and worked in New York City.

PAULINA. (d. 1867). *Northern Paiute.* The Walpapi and Yahuskin bands of Northern Paiutes were known as Snake Indians because of their location near the Snake River in Nevada, Oregon, and Idaho. They gave their name to the Snake War, sometimes referred to as the Paiute War (but not to be confused with the Paiute War of 1860 in Nevada under Numaga). Attacks by Indians against the miners, ranches, and stagecoaches in the Great Basin led to the assignment of former Civil War troops to Fort Boise and other posts in the area. Lieutenant Colonel General George Crook took command in 1866 and began a series of small tracking patrols that kept the insurgents on the run. On the death of Paulina in April 1867, Weawea assumed command. He held out for another year and a half until June 1868, when he surrendered with 800 remaining followers.

PELTIER, LEONARD. (1944–). *Sioux-Chippewa.* Leonard Peltier was born in Grand Forks, North Dakota. He grew up on a number of reservations and in different cities. In Seattle, he was part owner of an auto shop. He became increasingly involved with civil rights and community action and eventually began working with the American Indian Movement (AIM) in various capacities, including fund-raising and security at ceremonies. He was known among his peers for his bravery and reliability. Following a shoot-out at the Pine Ridge Reservation in South Dakota in 1975, in which one Native American and two FBI agents were killed, Peltier hid out with other activists in Oregon and California. He eventually reached Canada and requested political asylum. He was arrested, and, after U.S. officials submitted two falsified affidavits, he was extradited and tried in Fargo, North Dakota. In an earlier trial at Cedar Rapids, Iowa, two defendants also present at the Pine Ridge incident had been acquitted. It is believed by legal scholars that anti-Indian sentiment in Fargo, adverse rulings by the judge, coerced testimony of witnesses, and manufactured evidence led to Leonard Peltier's conviction. He is now serving two life sentences. International human rights advocates consider him a political prisoner.

PETALESHARO ("chief of men"). (c. 1787–c. 1832). *Pawnee.* In 1816 or 1817, Petalesharo rescued a Comanche girl from the Morning Star Ceremony, in which she was to be sacrificed, offering himself in her place. He won the respect of his people for his courage and his stance against the powerful priests, and, on succeeding his father as principal chief of the Skidi Pawnees (Northern Pawnees) of Nebraska, he proved influential among many of the Pawnee bands.

POCAHONTAS ("my favorite daughter"). (c. 1595–1617). *Powhatan (Pamunkey).* Although the exact circumstances are unknown, legend has it that, in 1608, Pocahontas saved the life of Captain John Smith, leader of the Jamestown colonists. She supposedly intervened just before Chief Powhatan was about to behead his prisoner, although Smith, in his later published account, made no mention of her role. In 1612, Pocahontas was decoyed onto one of the English ships on the Potomac, taken to Jamestown, and held as a hostage to bargain for the freedom of prisoners. While there, she was converted to Christianity and baptized. She was also courted by a colonist John Rolfe, whom she married in 1613. In 1616, Pocahontas and Rolfe traveled to England, where she was received as a princess. She died there of a European disease.

PONTIAC. (c. 1720–1769). *Ottawa-Chippewa.* Pontiac, born in northern Ohio of an Ottawa father and Chippewa mother, believed that if the Great Lakes tribes united and won French support, they could drive the English from the Great Lakes region. A powerful orator, he traveled among tribes to urge Indian unity. Delaware Prophet offered his support. In May 1763, Pontiac and his followers began a siege of Fort Detroit. Other area tribes attacked posts throughout the Old Northwest. The French never delivered any help, and the Indian alliance suffered a number of defeats. In October, Pontiac called off the siege. During a trip to Cahokia, Illinois, Pontiac was killed by a Peoria (Illinois) Indian who was probably in the pay of the British.

POPÉ (El Popé, "pumpkin mountain"). (d. 1690). *Tewa.* Popé, a shaman of the San Juan Pueblo, refused to convert to Christianity despite a series of arrests by the Spanish. He planned a general uprising of Pueblo Indians, sending out runners among them. The attack came in August 1680. Warriors from numerous pueblos along the Rio Grande and to the west moved against soldiers and priests stationed among them, as well as against ranchers of outlying haciendas. About 500 rebels moved on Santa Fe and, after a week-long siege, captured the city, driving the Spanish back to Mexico. Popé, who suppressed all traces of Spanish culture among his people, became increasingly tyrannical. By the time he died, his alliance had all but dissolved, and, in 1692, the Spanish recaptured Santa Fe.

POUNDMAKER (Opeteca Hanawaywin). (c. 1842–1886). *Cree*. Poundmaker, although raised by the powerful Blackfoot chief Crowfoot, was recognized as a chief of the Plains Cree in 1878. As such, he led his warriors in support of the Metis in the Second Riel Rebellion. In March 1885, he led an attack on the town of Battleford on the North Saskatchewan River. With military pressure and the surrender of Louis Riel, Poundmaker and his warriors surrendered at Battleford in June. Along with Big Bear, who held out until early July, Poundmaker was sentenced to three years imprisonment. He was given an early release the next year, but, suffering from poor health, died while on a visit to Crowfoot's Blackfoot Indian Reserve in Alberta.

POWHATAN (Wahunsonacock). (c. 1547–1618). *Powhatan (Pamunkey)*. Although the name Powhatan was a place name and village name, Chief Wahunsonacock became known to the English by it. His father had founded the powerful alliance of Algonquian-speaking Tidewater tribes, and Powhatan had further strengthened it into a confederacy of 32 bands and about 200 villages. His primary village was Werowacomoco on the north bank of the York River. In fall 1608, after Powhatan had released him (according to legend, at the request of Pocahontas), Captain John Smith crowned Powhatan as "king" of the region in a political maneuver to appease him. Four years after Powhatan's death, his brother Opechancanough led the confederacy in an uprising against the English.

QUANAH PARKER. (c. 1847–1911). *Comanche*. Quanah Parker's mother Cynthia Parker had been kidnapped by Comanches as a nine-year-old in 1836, and had become the devoted wife of the Comanche chief Peta Nocono of the Nocono band. Their son Quanah proved himself in battle as a teenager and became a war chief among the powerful Kwahadie band in 1867. He and his followers resisted the reservation life during the 1860s and 1870s. His warriors were the last to surrender in the Red River War of 1874–75. Quanah adapted to life on the reservation, learning English and Spanish. By 1878, he was a spokesman for the Kwahadie band, and, by 1890, principal chief of all the Comanche bands. He also played a major role in spreading knowledge of the ritual use of the peyote plant among Plains Indians.

RED BIRD (Wanig Suchka). (c. 1788–1828). *Winnebago*. Red Bird was chief of the Winnebagos living at Prairie La Crosse near the Wisconsin-Illinois border. During the 1820s, with lead prices rising, more and more miners poured into the region. Hostilities arose, including the Indian attack on a keelboat in June 1827 to rescue kidnapped women. With the subsequent show of force by volunteer miners as well as regulars under General Henry Atkinson, Red Bird surrendered. He died of dysentery while awaiting trial for the death of settlers. In August 1829, Winnebago chiefs signed a treaty at Prairie du Chien ceding all tribal lands in Illinois and Wisconsin located south of the Fox and Wisconsin rivers.

RED CLOUD (Mahpiua Luta, "scarlet cloud"). (c. 1822–1909). *Oglala Sioux*. Red Cloud was born near the forks of the Platte River in Nebraska. He was not a hereditary chief, but, because of bravery in battle and leadership qualities, he rose to be head chief of his band. During the 1860s, miners began settling in the homelands of the Sioux in Montana and Wyoming, violating the terms of the Fort Laramie Treaty of 1851. The opening of a direct route between Montana and the Oregon Trail in Wyoming brought traffic over Sioux hunting grounds and led to the War for the Bozeman Trail in 1866–68. In the Fort Laramie Treaty of 1868, the Great Sioux Reservation was created, and the army evacuated the region. When the Sioux again went to war in the War for the Black Hills of 1875–76 under Sitting Bull, Red Cloud kept his band at peace. During the Ghost Dance Uprising of 1890, he again advocated peace with whites.

RED EAGLE (Lumhe Chati; William Weatherford). (c. 1780–1824). *Creek*. Red Eagle, or William Weatherford, the son of a Scottish trader and Creek woman, was raised among the Creeks in Alabama. U.S. expansion in Creek territory led to the tribe's polarization into war and peace factions. Some of the war faction fought alongside the English in the War of 1812. Red Eagle and others carried out raids in their homeland. In August 1813, he led an attack on Fort Mims on the confluence of the Alabama and Tombigbee rivers. Federal and state troops were mobilized, leading to the defeat of the Creeks at the Horseshoe Bend of the Tallapoosa River by General Andrew Jackson in March 1814. Red Eagle surrendered soon afterward and agreed to work for peace. In a follow-up series of negotiations, Creek leaders were coerced into signing the Treaty of Fort Jackson, which took away 23 million acres of tribal lands.

RIEL, LOUIS DAVID (Louis Riel, Jr.). (1844–1885). *Metis*. Louis Riel was born at the Red River Settlement in Canada, the son of the Frenchman Louis Riel and the French-Chippewa Julie Lagimodiere. His people were known as Metis, "mixed-blood" in French, many of them of French-Cree ancestry. Like many of the Metis, Louis was provided with a Catholic education, but learned Indian customs as well. Since trade with Americans was limited by the Canadian government and their land rights violated by Protestant settlers, the Metis under Riel's leadership attempted to achieve independence in the First Riel Rebellion of 1869. They won concessions in the Manitoba Act, but settlers continued encroaching on their territory. Many Metis decided to move westward to the Saskatchewan River near the buffalo of the Great Plains. The pattern repeated itself with Metis rights ignored, largely as a result of the building of the Canadian Pacific Railway, and Riel was asked to return from the United States to lead the Second Riel Rebellion (or the North-West Rebellion) of 1885. He surrendered soon after defeat at the hands of the North West Field Force. He was tried, sentenced to death, and executed.

ROMAN NOSE (Woquini). (1830–1868). *Cheyenne*. Roman Nose was possibly born among the Northern Cheyennes, but established his place in history among the Southern branch of the tribe, fighting alongside Southern Cheyenne chiefs of the famous Dog Soldiers military society, such as Bull Bear, Tall Bull, and White Horse. In 1868–69, because of Cheyenne raids following the attack on Black Kettle's peaceful band at Sand Creek, General Philip Sheridan launched what is known as the Sheridan Campaign into Kansas and Colorado. In an engagement of the Southern Plains War, the Battle of Beecher's Island, named after Lieutenant Frederick Beecher, Roman Nose was killed.

ROSS, JOHN (Coowescoowe, "the egret"). (1790–1866). *Cherokee*. John Ross was born along the Coosa River in Georgia, his father Scottish and his mother Cherokee. He supported U.S. forces in the Creek War of 1813–14. After the war, Ross became increasingly involved in Cherokee affairs. He helped found the Cherokee Nation, with a written constitution and a republican government. But the Indian Removal Act of 1830 called for the relocation of eastern tribes to an Indian Territory west of the Mississippi. In 1830–38, Ross headed numerous delegations to Washington, D.C., to argue the case for his people remaining on their ancestral homelands. Despite the fact that Ross argued and won the Cherokee case before the Supreme Court, President Andrew Jackson called for Cherokee removal. After the Trail of Tears in 1838–39, Ross continued in his capacity as a leader and spokesman for his people.

SACAJAWEA (Sacagawea, "birdwoman"). (c. 1784–c. 1812 or 1884). *Shoshone.* Sacajawea was born in the 1780s among the Lemhi Shoshones of central Idaho and western Montana. While a teenager, she was kidnapped by Hidatsas, who took her to North Dakota. In 1804, she was purchased (or won in a gambling match) by French-Canadian trader Toussaint Charbonneau. Lewis and Clark, having left St. Louis in May 1804, spent the following winter in the Mandan villages on the Missouri, where they hired Charbonneau and Sacajawea. Sacajawea, the only female member of the expedition, a new baby in a cradleboard on her back, acted as guide, interpreter, and diplomat for Lewis and Clark. In Montana, she was reunited with her brother Cameahwait now chief of his band, and was able to attain horses and supplies. The expedition reached the Pacific Ocean in November 1805. On the return trip, Sacajawea and Charbonneau left the expedition at the Hidatsa village at the mouth of the Knife River. Lewis and Clark returned to St. Louis in 1806. It is not known for certain when or where Sacajawea died. One version has it that after she and Charbonneau visited St. Louis in 1809 and left their son with Clark to be educated, then traveled up the Missouri with trader Manuel Lisa, where she died from disease in 1812. In another version, she lived for a time with Comanches, then returned to her homeland, settling among Wind River Shoshones in Wyoming and dying when she was about 100 years old.

SASSACUS ("he is wild"). (c. 1560–1637). *Pequot.* Sassacus became grand sachem of the Pequots about 1632 on the death of his father. The warlike Pequots resisted white expansion; a branch tribe, the Mohegans, broke off from the Pequots under Uncas and became allies of the colonists. In the Pequot War of 1636–37, Sassacus led his people in revolt against the New England colonists. Armies under captains John Mason and John Underhill moved against the Pequots and destroyed their village on the Mystic River in Connecticut. Sassacus went into hiding, but was killed by Mohawks.

SATANTA (White Bear). (1830–1878). *Kiowa.* At the time of the death of principal chief Little Mountain in 1866, Satanta headed the war faction, and Kicking Bird the peace faction; Lone Wolf was selected as the compromise choice as principal chief over both of them. Satanta spoke at the Medicine Lodge council in 1867 and became known as the "Orator of the Plains" among whites. He participated with Lone Wolf, Mamanti, Satank, and other militants in the Kiowa Wars of the 1860s-70s. Satanta was sentenced to death for an attack on a wagon train. Humanitarian groups protested the harsh sentence, and he was imprisoned at Huntsville, Texas, for life. Four years into his sentence he committed suicide by jumping from a window.

SEQUOYAH (Sogwali, "sparrow"; George Guess). (c. 1770–1843). *Cherokee.* Sequoyah was born in Tennessee of a Cherokee mother and possibly a white father. As a boy of 12, he moved to Alabama with his mother. Sequoyah served under Andrew Jackson in the Creek War of 1813–14. After the war, in 1818, he and his family emigrated to Arkansas as part of Chief John Jolly's band. Before moving, in 1809, he had started work on a written version of the Cherokee language. He eventually reduced the Cherokee language to 86 characters representing all the different sounds, finishing his project in 1821. In 1829, Sequoyah moved from Arkansas with his wife and children to the Indian Territory. As President of the Western Cherokees, he helped unite Eastern and Western factions in the 1839 Cherokee Act of Union. In 1842, he organized an expedition to locate through a study of Indian speech patterns a lost band of Cherokees who had migrated west during the American Revolution. The trip through the Southwest aggravated his already poor health, and he died in Mexico.

SITTING BULL (Tatanka Yotanka). (c. 1831–1890). *Hunkpapa Sioux.* Sitting Bull was born along the Grand River in South Dakota, the son of a chief. When Santee Sioux hid out in the Dakotas in 1863–64 during the Minnesota Uprising, Sitting Bull offered them support with raids on army scouting parties. While the War for the Bozeman Trail of 1866–68 involving Red Cloud's Oglalas raged in the Powder River country, Sitting Bull led raids to the north. Sitting Bull came to be recognized as a spiritual leader and was eventually made head of the war council. Crazy Horse, Gall, and other leaders were among his lieutenants in the War for the Black Hills in 1876–77. After the war, Sitting Bull and some of his followers headed for Canada, but the Canadian government refused to provide supplies. The Sioux chief surrendered to the U.S. Army in 1881. He was held as a prisoner for two years before being allowed to settle on the Standing Rock Reservation in North Dakota. In 1885–86, he toured with Buffalo Bill Cody's Wild West Show. In 1890, Sitting Bull invited his nephew Kicking Bear to Standing Rock to demonstrate the Ghost Dance. The Indian agent accused Sitting Bull of inciting the Sioux to militancy and ordered his arrest during which Sitting Bull was killed.

SLOCUM, JOHN (Squ-sacht-un). (fl. 1880s). *Squakson (Coast Salish).* John Slocum learned Christian tenets from missionaries in the Puget Sound region of Washington. In 1881, he claimed that while in a trance he was transported to heaven where he received instructions on how to bring about Indian salvation, and he founded *Tschadam,* known to whites as the Indian Shaker Religion, which spread throughout the region.

SMOHALLA ("the preacher"). (c.1815–1907). *Wanapam.* Smohalla was a Wanapam Indian of the same Sahaptin language family as the Nez Perces. He lived along the upper Columbia River in eastern Washington. As a young man, he gained renown as a warrior. Drawing on the teachings of Catholic missionaries and other Indian prophets, he began to preach his own revelations about 1850. A rivalry with the nearby Sinkiuse chief Moses led to confrontation on a battlefield. Smohalla was wounded and left for dead. He departed the area and traveled for several years, as far south as Mexico, then back overland through Nevada. He claimed he had visited the Spirit World and had been sent back to teach his people. Because of his message countering white influences and white use of Indian lands, he was arrested several times.

SPOTTED TAIL (Sinte Galeshka). (c. 1833-1881). *Brule Sioux.* Spotted Tail was born either along the White River in South Dakota (or possibly near Fort Laramie in Wyoming). In the Grattan Affair of 1854, Spotted Tail participated in the attack on soldiers and also fought at Blue Water Creek (Ash Hollow) the next year. In order to prevent further hostilities against his people, he gave himself up at Fort Laramie, chanting his death song. The army soon released him. Because of his courage, the Brule council passed over a hereditary chief in his favor. By the 1860s, Spotted Tail was chief spokesman for all the Brule bands. During the War for the Bozeman Trail of 1866-68, he counseled accommodation with whites. He was one of the signers of the Fort Laramie Treaty of 1868, establishing the Great Sioux Reservation. During the War for the Black Hills of 1875-76, the Brule leader helped negotiate the surrender of Sioux militants. Some of the Sioux never forgave him for the consequences, especially the death of Crazy Horse, and plotted his overthrow. In a dispute over a woman at the Rosebud Reservation in South Dakota, Crow Dog shot and killed Spotted Tail.

SQUANTO (Tisquantum). (c. 1580–1622). *Wampanoag.* Squanto of the Patuxet band of Wampanoags is thought to have been kidnapped from his homeland on Cape Cod, Massachusetts, by an English trading ship in 1605 (or perhaps later) and taken to Europe. He managed to return to North America in 1619. His knowledge of English enabled him to act as translator between the Wampanoag grand sachem Massasoit and the Pilgrims. He also helped instruct the Pilgrims in planting and fertilizing techniques. He died of a European disease, probably smallpox.

STANDING BEAR (Mo-chu-no-zhi). (c. 1829–1908). *Ponca.* In 1877, the Poncas were forcibly removed from their homeland on the Niobrara River in Nebraska to the Indian Territory. After relocation, many of the tribe died, including Chief Standing Bear's son. Standing Bear wanted to bury the boy in his ancestral homeland and set out from the Indian Territory with an escort of 30 warriors. The party was intercepted, however, and detained in Omaha. Standing Bear gained the support of non-Indian reformers for his plight, and lawyers volunteered their services. They applied for a writ of habeas corpus on the Ponca's behalf. Federal attorneys argued that Indians were not persons under the terms of the Constitution and not entitled to habeas corpus. The judge ruled, however, that Standing Bear was indeed a person under the law with inalienable rights. The Poncas were later granted a permanent home in Nebraska.

STANISLAUS (Estanislao). (fl. 1820s). *Mission Indian (probably Yokuts).* Stanislaus, captured when young, was raised and educated at the San Jose Mission in California. He became dissatisfied with the treatment of his people and led an escape in 1827 or 1828. With another leader, Cipriano, he organized the Indians of the northern San Joaquin Valley into general resistance. The rebels repelled two Mexican expeditions. A third expedition was organized, including about 100 soldiers plus Indian auxiliaries. Artillery fire breached the rebels' defenses, but Stanislaus and others avoided capture through a system of tunnels. Stanislaus fled to San Jose, where he was offered refuge by priests. He was later pardoned for the uprising.

TALLCHIEF, MARIA. (1925–). *Osage.* Maria Tallchief was born in Fairfax, Oklahoma. In 1842–47, she was a soloist with Ballet Russe de Monte Carlo; in 1948–49, she danced with the American Ballet Theatre. For the most of her remaining career, she danced with the New York City Ballet, becoming a prima ballerina. She was married to George Ballanchine, the choreographer, from 1946 to 1952. In 1966, she stopped performing and began teaching dance.

TASCALUSA (Tuscaluca, "black warrior"). (fl. 1540s). *Alabama.* Contacts between the Alabama, or Alibamu, Indians and Hernando de Soto's conquistadors in Alabama proved peaceful until the Spanish demanded supplies and burden carriers from the Indians. The chieftain Tascalusa called his warriors to his village. When the soldiers tried to arrest Tascalusa, fighting erupted. The Battle of Mabila on October 18, 1540, lasted all day, but Spanish guns proved too much for the native peoples, and the village was destroyed. It is not known what happened to Tascalusa. His son's body was found among the dead.

TECUMSEH (Shooting Star). (c. 1768–1813). *Shawnee.* Tecumseh was probably born in the Shawnee village of Piqua near present-day Springfield, Ohio. In 1795, he refused to sign the Treaty of Fort Greenville, which forced the tribes of the Old Northwest to cede huge tracts of territory. Tecumseh maintained that no single Indian or tribe had the right to give up lands to whites because the lands belonged to all Indians and tribes. In a second treaty at Fort Greenville in 1809, William Henry Harrison, the governor of Indian Territory, forced additional cessions. Tecumseh, repudiating the validity of the treaties, called for an Indian nation extending from Canada to the Gulf of Mexico. While Tecumseh was away on a trip to gather support, his brother Tenskwatawa, the Shawnee Prophet, ordered a premature attack on Harrison's militia force, and the Indians were routed. In 1811, Harrison's army marched on Prophetstown in Indiana and burned the village to the ground. The defeat broke the momentum of Tecumseh's military alliance. In the War of 1812 between the United States and England, Tecumseh was commissioned a brigadier general in charge of some 2,000 warriors from various tribes. At the Battle of the Thames in Ontario, he was killed.

TEKAKWITHA, KATERI (Catherine Tekakwitha; Lily of the Mohawks). (1656–1680). *Mohawk.* Kateri grew up in the village of Caughnawaga on the Mohawk River near present-day Fonda, New York, raised by her uncle. Against her uncle's wishes, she was converted to Christianity by Jesuit missionaries. In 1677, she fled to Canada with Christianized Oneidas who had visited her people. Kateri settled at Sault St. Louis near Montreal. She was allowed to make a vow of chastity and become a nun. In 1884, Kateri became a candidate for canonization by the Roman Catholic Church; in 1943, she was declared venerable; then, in 1980, she was declared blessed, the second step towards sainthood.

TENSKWATAWA ("the open door"; Shawnee Prophet). (1775–1836). *Shawnee.* Bother of Tecumseh. Tenskwatawa led a dissolute life as a young man, but found himself as a prophet. In 1805, he experienced a deep trance after which he declared he had visited the spirit world and received a message from the Master of Life. Tenskwatawa preached a return to traditional Indian ways, such as community ownership of property. He also claimed he had received the power to cure disease and prevent death on the battlefield. At the former Miami village of Tippecanoe in Indiana, he and his brother established the intertribal community of Prophetstown. Tenskwatawa's defeat by troops under William Henry Harrison while Tecumseh was on a trip, led to the break-up of the Indian alliance and an estrangement of the brothers. Tenskwatawa moved to Canada. He eventually headed to Missouri then Kansas with relocated Shawnees.

THORPE, JIM (James Thorpe; Bright Path). (1888-1953). *Sac.* Jim Thorpe was born near Prague, Oklahoma. In 1907, he entered the Carlisle Indian School in Pennsylvania. Coached by Glenn ("Pop") Warner and playing halfback, Thorpe led the Carlisle football team in upsets over Army, Harvard, and other schools. At the 1912 Olympics in Stockholm, Sweden, Thorpe won gold medals in the pentathlon and decathlon. The next year, he was forced to surrender his medals because, in 1909-10, he had played semiprofessional baseball for a North Carolina team. Thorpe later played professional baseball with the New York Giants and football with the Canton (Ohio) Bulldogs, then went on to become the supervisor of recreation for Chicago parks. His Olympic medals were reinstated in 1983.

TILOUKAIKT. (d. 1849). *Cayuse.* Tiloukaikt and other Cayuse leaders allowed the building of a Presbyterian mission in their homeland in the Walla Walla Valley of Oregon. Some also sent their children to the school at Waiilatpu to be taught by the missionary Marcus Whitman and his wife Narcissa. With many Indian dying from diseases, Tiloukaikt became suspicious that the missionaries were poisoning them with medicine. During a measles epidemic in 1847, ill-feeling boiled over. While Tiloukaikt was visiting the mission, he had words with Whitman. A Cayuse by the name of Tomahas struck Whitman from behind, killing him. Others joined the violence, killing Narcissa and 12 others. The settlers in the Willamette Valley raised a volunteer militia, which attacked an encampment of innocent Cayuses. Warriors from other tribes joined the uprising. Tiloukaikt and Tomahas, plus three other Cayuses, tired of hiding, turned themselves in two years later. They were taken to Oregon City, tried hastily, and sentenced to hang. Before dying, Tiloukaikt refused Presbyterian rites, accepting Catholic ones instead.

TURK (El Turco). (d. 1541). Probably *Pawnee.* The Turk was a slave at Pecos Pueblo in New Mexico when Francisco de Coronado's expedition out of Mexico came to the region. The Spanish gave him his name because of his style of headdress. He described to Coronado the abundance of gold to the north, perhaps hoping for an escort back to his homeland. In 1541, along with the Turk and another Indian known as Ysopete, Coronado departed the Rio Grande with his army of conquistadors. The Turk led the Spaniards to the barren Staked Plain of Texas. Convinced that the guide was trying to trick him, Coronado had him placed in irons. The expedition crossed Kansas, and, at the Kansas River, sent messengers ahead to summon the Pawnees. The Turk tried to instigate an attack by the Pawnees and was killed by the Spanish. Coronado returned to Spain without the Turk's promised gold.

VICTORIO (Beduiat). (c.1825–1880). *Mimbreno Apache.* As a young warrior, Victorio fought under Mangas Coloradas. On the death of the latter in 1863, Victorio assumed leadership of the Mimbrenos. Other Apache bands joined his band. They came to be known collectively as Ojo Caliente or Warm Springs Apaches, since their agency was located at Ojo Caliente (Warm Springs) in southwest New Mexico. During the 1860s-70s, the band carried out numerous raids in New Mexico and Texas. Victorio agreed to cease hostilities if granted a permanent reservation at Warm

Springs, but negotiations failed and he and his followers were ordered to the San Carlos Reservation in Arizona among Chiricahua bands. A period of violence started, with the Apaches carrying out raids in Arizona, New Mexico, Texas, and Mexico. Both the United States and Mexico mobilized forces. Victorio, a master tactician, eluded them all. In October 1880, while fleeing both American and Mexican detachments, the rebels were attacked by a force of 350 Mexicans and Tarahumara Indians under Colonel Joaquin Terrazas. Only about 30 warriors survived the two-day battle of Tres Castillos ("Three Peaks"). Victorio turned up among the dead.

WALKARA (Wakara, Walker, "yellow"). (c. 1808–1855). *Ute.* Walkara, one of five sons of a chief of the Timpanogos band, was born along the Spanish Fork River in what is now Utah. He established his reputation as a warrior and horseman and gathered a band, including some Paiutes and Shoshones, who carried out raids on ranches and travelers in the Great Basin region and along the Old Spanish Trail between New Mexico and California. He earned the reputation in California as "the greatest horse thief in history." After Mormon settlement in the Great Basin, Walkara established a trade relationship with Brigham Young. But hostilities arose between Indians and whites. In 1853, Walkara began regular raids on Mormon settlements. During the so-called Walker War, Brigham Young had the settlers move from their outlying farms and ranches into forts. Their defense proved successful, and Walkara agreed to peace before winter.

WATIE, STAND (Degataga, "immovable"). (1806–1871). *Cherokee.* Born in Georgia, Stand Watie was educated at mission schools, then returned to his homeland to work with his brother Elias Boudinot on the newspaper *Cherokee Phoenix.* Accepting the view that resistance to white expansion in the South was hopeless, Stand Watie became an active member of the pro-removal Treaty Party, led by his uncle and cousin, Major and John Ridge. He was one of the signers of the Treaty of New Echota in 1835. After the Trail of Tears to the Indian Territory, Stand Watie was marked for assassination, along with his brother and the Ridges, by members of the Ross Party; he was the only one of the four to escape. In 1861, when the Cherokees gave up neutrality and supported the Confederacy, Stand Watie organized a regiment of cavalry and was commissioned as a colonel of the First Cherokee Mounted Rifles. He is famous for his role in the Battle of Pea Ridge, Arkansas, in March 1862, in which his men captured the Union artillery and covered the retreat of Confederate soldiers. Watie was promoted to brigadier general and fought in the Indian Territory, Arkansas, Missouri, Kansas, and Texas. He surrendered to the Union in June 1865 in the Indian Territory, the last general in the Confederate army to do so. During the war, in 1864, he was elected principal chief of the Southern band of Cherokees.

WOVOKA ("the cutter"; Jack Wilson). (c.1856–1932). *Northern Paiute.* Wovoka was born along the Walker River in Mason Valley, Nevada. He is thought to have been the son of the prophet Tavibo. In any case, he grew up in the same area as the earlier Paiute shaman and was influenced by his teachings, as well as those of other reservation prophets, such as Smohalla and John Slocum. For part of his youth, he lived with the Wilson family, who were devout Christians. In late 1888, Wovoka became sick with a fever. On recovery, he claimed that he had been taken to the spirit world for a visit with the Supreme Being. He founded a new version of the Ghost Dance. The religion spread to reservation Indians throughout the West. Some of his followers came to consider Wovoka as the Messiah, and he was sometimes referred to as the "Red Man's Christ." After the Wounded Knee Massacre in 1890, Wovoka, shocked by the bloodshed, called for peace with whites.

FAMOUS BATTLES AND INCIDENTS

(See map of "Famous Battles")

Pequot War: On May 26, 1637, colonists under Captain John Mason and Captain John Underhill kill more than 500 men, women, and children in an attack on Sassacus's village of Pequots at Mystic, Connecticut.

Pavonia Massacre (Slaughter of the Innocents): On February 25–26, 1643, director general of New Netherland Willem Kieft sends soldiers to attack Wappinger refugees, mostly women and children, at Pavonia on the Hudson River in New York.

Powhatan Wars (Jamestown Wars): On March 22, 1622, Opechancanough's Powhatans attack the Jamestown Colony's tobacco fields in Virginia. On April 18, 1644, Opechancanough orders an attack on settlements along the James River.

King Philip's War: On December 19, 1675, in the Great Swamp Fight, colonists under Plymouth governor Josiah Winslow attack Canonchet's village of Narragansets near Kingston, Rhode Island, killing about 600 men, women, and children.

Pueblo Rebellion: On August 10, 1680, Indians of various Rio Grande pueblos united under the Tewa shaman Popé attack the Spanish in New Mexico. On August 14–21, rebels lay siege to Santa Fe, driving Spanish back to Mexico.

French and Indian War: On July 9, 1755, French troops and Indian allies, among them Algonkins, Lenni Lenapes (Delawares), Ottawas, Shawnees, and Wyandots (Hurons), defeat Major General Edward Braddock's column heading for Fort Duquesne (Pittsburgh) in western Pennsylvania. On September 8, 1755, at Lake George in New York, the French under Jean-Armand, Baron de Dieskau, are defeated by English troops under William Johnson with Mohawk allies under Hendrick. Hendrick is killed.

Pontiac's Rebellion: From May 9 to October 21, 1763, warriors from among allied Ottawas, Chippewas, Illinois, Kickapoos, Lenni Lenapes (Delawares), Miamis, Potawatomis, Senecas, Shawnees, and Wyandots (Hurons) hold a siege of Fort Detroit. That same period, raids are carried out throughout the Old Northwest. On August 5–6, 1763, at Bushy Run, Lieutenant Colonel Henry Bouquet's relief column to the British garrison at Fort Pitt (Pittsburgh) defeats Lenni Lenapes, Mingos (Iroquois), Shawnees, and Wyandots.

Paxton Riots: On December 27, 1763, Scottish-Irish Presbyterians out of Paxton, Pennsylvania, known as the "Paxton Boys," attack and kill 14 missionized Conestoga Indians (Susquehannocks), previously placed in a public workhouse for their protection.

Lord Dunmore's War: On October 10, 1774, at Point Pleasant in West Virginia, Shawnees under Cornstalk, plus allied Lenni Lenapes, Mingos, and Wyandots, are driven back by militia forces under Brigadier General Andrew Lewis.

American Revolution: On August 6, 1777, at Oriskany in New York, Mohawks led by Joseph Brant (Thayendanegea) and Senecas led by Cornplanter, along with Onondagas, fight against their former allies the Oneidas and Tuscaroras, who support a militia force under General Nicholas Herkimer, with heavy casualties on both sides. On November 11, 1778, at Cherry Valley in New York, Mohawks under Joseph Brant, Senecas under Little Beard and Gucinges, and Tory troops under Captain Walter Butler attack settlers. On August 29, 1779, at Newtown near present-day Elmira, New York, Tories under Colonel William Butler, Mohawks under Joseph Brant, and Senecas under Old Smoke fight to a standoff with troops of the Sullivan-Clinton Campaign, sent out by General George Washington. On March 8–9, 1782, because a plate is stolen, Patriots under Colonel David Williamson attack missionized Moravian Indians (Lenni Lenapes) at Gnaddenhutten in Ohio.

Miami War (Little Turtle's War): On October 19–21, 1790, General Josiah Harmar's force is defeated on the Maumee River in Indiana by allied tribes (Chippewas, Lenni Lenapes, Mingos, Ottawas, Potawatomis, Shawnees, and Wyandots) under the Miami chief Little Turtle, the Lenni Lenape Buckongahelas, and the Shawnees Blue Jacket and Catahecassa. On November 4, 1791, Arthur St. Clair's force is defeated on the upper Wabash in Indiana. On August 20, 1794, at Fallen Timbers near Fort Miami in Ohio, troops under "Mad" Anthony Wayne defeat the allied tribes.

Tecumseh's Rebellion: On November 7, 1811, at Tippecanoe (Prophetstown) in Indiana, while the Shawnee leader Tecumseh is on a trip south, his brother Tenskwatawa and allied Indians are routed by troops under General William Henry Harrison.

Creek War: On August 30, 1813, Creeks under Red Eagle (William Weatherford) take Fort Mims in Alabama. On March 27, 1814, at Horseshoe Bend, the Creeks are defeated by forces under General Andrew Jackson plus Cherokee allies.

War of 1812: On October 5, 1813, at the Thames River in Ontario, American forces under General William Henry Harrison defeat British forces under Colonel Henry Proctor. Tecumseh, previously commissioned a brigadier general in charge of British-allied Indians, is killed.

Black Hawk War: On May 14, 1832, at Stillman's Run in Illinois, allied Sacs and Foxes under the Sac chief Black Hawk rout a militia force under Major Isaac Stillman. On July 21, 1832, at the Battle of Wisconsin Heights near Sauk City in Wisconsin, an advance party of General Henry Atkinson's troops defeat Black Hawk's and White Cloud's (Winnebago Prophet) followers. On August 1–3, 1832, at the Bad Axe River in Wisconsin, federal and militia troops kill as many as 300 Indians, many of them as they attempt to swim to safety across the Mississippi.

Second Seminole War: On December 28, 1835, while Osceola leads an attack on Indian agent Wiley Thompson, other Seminole militants ambush Major Francis Dade's column on its way to reinforce Fort King in Florida. On New Year's Eve, at Withlacoochee

River, Osceola leads attack on the camp of General Duncan Clinch. Osceola is captured at a supposed peace council near St. Augustine on October 21, 1837, and dies in prison the next year. In seven years of fighting, nine commanders in chief are unable to defeat the Seminoles, who hide out in the Everglades. On December 25, 1837, at Lake Okeechobee, freedom fighters under Alligator, Arpeika, and Wild Cat battle troops of Colonel Zachary Taylor to a standoff.

Cayuse War: On November 29, 1847, Tiloukaikt and Tomahas, believing that Cayuse children sick with measles have been poisoned, attack and kill Presbyterian missionary Marcus Whitman, his wife Narcissa, and 12 others at Waiilatpu in Washington.

Grattan Affair: On August 19, 1854, troops under Lieutenant John Grattan, responding to a report of a Sioux named High Forehead shooting an arrow at a Mormon's livestock, attack a party of Brule Sioux near Fort Laramie in Wyoming and kill chief Conquering Bear; the soldiers are in turn wiped out. On September 3, 1855, at Ash Hollow (Blue Water Creek) in Nebraska, troops under General William S. Harney defeat the Brule Sioux now under Little Thunder.

Yakima War: On July 17, 1856, at Grande Ronde Valley (Oregon), volunteers under Lieutenant Colonel G.B. Shaw defeat Wallawalla, Cayuse, and Umatilla allies of the Yakima chief Kamiakin.

Rogue River War: On May 27–28, 1856, at Big Meadows in Oregon, Takelmas and Tututnis under Old John attack troops led by Captain Andrew Jackson Smith, then scatter.

Solomon Fork: On July 29, 1857, at Solomon Fork in Kansas, troops under Lieutenant Colonel Edwin V. Sumner pursue Southern Cheyennes.

Coeur d'Alene War (Spokane War): On September 1–5, 1858, at Four Lakes and Spokane Plain in Washington, allied tribes (Coeur d'Alenes, Spokanes, Palouses, and Yakimas) under the Yakima chief Kamiakin are defeated by troops led by Colonel George Wright.

Paiute War (Pyramid Lake War): On May 12, 1860, at Big Bend in the Truckee River Valley in Nevada, Paiutes under Numaga ambush Nevada volunteers led by Major William Ormsby.

Apache Resistance: In the Bascom Affair, on February 4, 1861, Lieutenant George Bascom tries to arrest the Chiricahua Apache chief Cochise for a crime he denies committing, leading to a decade of Apache militancy under Cochise and Mimbreno Mangas Coloradas in Arizona and New Mexico. On July 15, 1862, at Apache Pass in New Mexico, troops out of California under Colonel James Carleton repel Apache militants.

Santee Sioux (Minnesota Uprising): On August 20, 1862, Santees attack the settlement of New Ulm in Minnesota; on August 21, Fort Ridgely; and, on August 23, New Ulm again. On September 2, in the Battle of Birch Coulee, and on September 23, in the Battle of Wood Lake, troops under General Henry H. Sibley scatter the rebels. The largest mass public execution in U.S. history takes place on December 26, 1862, when 38 Santees are hanged, some of them mistakenly identified for violence at New Ulm. The fighting spreads to North Dakota the next two years and involves the Yankton Sioux as well. On July 24, 1863, Sibley engages militants at Big Mound; on July 26, at Dead Buffalo Lake; and, on July 28, at Stony Lake. On September 3, 1863, General Alfred

Sully engages allied Sioux at Whitestone Hill; and, on July 28, 1864, at Killdeer Mountain.

Shoshone Uprising (Bear River Campaign): Colonel Patrick E. Connor leads the Bear River Campaign of California volunteers out of Fort Douglas against Bear Hunter's village in Utah, defeating the Shoshones on January 27, 1863.

Navajo War: In the summer of 1863, Christopher "Kit" Carson, sent into field by General James Carleton, leads scorched-earth campaign, destroying much of the Navajos' livestock and grain. On January 12–15, 1864, Carson traps militants under Manuelito at Canyon de Chelly in Arizona.

Carson Campaign: On November 25, 1864, at Adobe Walls in the Texas Panhandle, troops under Kit Carson destroy the encampment of Little Mountain's Kiowas plus Comanche allies.

Cheyenne-Arapaho War: On November 29, 1864, at Sand Creek near Fort Lyon in Colorado, Colonel John Chivington's Colorado volunteers attack peace chief Black Kettle's encampment, killing about 200 men, women, and children.

Powder River Expedition: On August 29, 1865, at the Tongue River in Wyoming, General Patrick E. Connor's men destroy Black Bear's Northern Arapaho encampment.

War for the Bozeman Trail (Red Cloud's War): On December 21, 1866, in the Fetterman Fight, Captain William J. Fetterman's men are killed near Fort Phil Kearny in Montana by Sioux under Crazy Horse. On August 2, 1867, in the Wagon Box Fight, a wood-cutting detail out of the fort is routed by the Sioux.

Southern Plains War (Sheridan Campaign): On September 17, 1868, during the Sheridan Campaign, at Beecher's Island in Colorado, Southern Cheyenne Dog Soldiers and Sioux warriors are repelled by troops of the Sheridan Campaign under Major George Forsyth. Lieutenant Beecher is killed, as is the Cheyenne war chief Roman Nose. On November 27, 1868, at Washita in the Indian Territory (Oklahoma), Lieutenant Colonel George Armstrong Custer attacks Black Kettle's Southern Cheyenne encampment, killing the peace chief and more than 100 others. On December 25, 1868, at Soldier Spring in the Indian Territory, troops under Major Andrew Evans destroy a Comanche and Kiowa camp. On July 11, 1869, at Summit Springs in Colorado, Tall Bull and his Dog Soldiers are defeated by the 5th Cavalry.

Camp Grant Massacre: On April 30, 1971, at Camp Grant in Arizona, settlers out of Tucson attack Eskiminzin's peaceful band of Aravaipa Apaches, killing as many as 150.

Tonto Basin Campaign: On December 28, 1872, at Skull Canyon in Arizona, captains William Brown and James Burn defeat Apaches and Yavapais. On March 27, 1873, at Turret Peak, Captain George Randall is victorious.

Modoc War: On January 17, 1873, at the Stronghold (Lava Beds) in California, Modocs under Kintpuash (Captain Jack) repel California and Colorado volunteers. General Edward Canby leads ensuing campaign. The Modoc woman Winema arranges a peace council on April 11, but Modocs kill Canby and a peace commissioner. Kintpuash and three other Modocs are later hanged.

Red River War: On June 27, 1874, at Adobe Walls in the Texas Panhandle, Quanah Parker's followers are repelled by the repeater rifles of buffalo hunters. On September 28, 1874, at Palo Duro Canyon in Texas, troops under Colonel Ranald S. Mackenzie destroy a Comanche and Kiowa encampment.

Sioux War for the Black Hills: On March 17, 1876, at the Powder River in Montana, Crazy Horse's warriors fight troops under Colonel Joseph Reynolds. On June 17, 1876, at the Rosebud in Montana, warriors under Crazy Horse and Gall repel troops under General George Crook. On June 25, 1876, at the Little Bighorn in Montana, Lieutenant George Armstrong Custer's men are wiped out by Sioux and Cheyennes under Sitting Bull, Crazy Horse, and Gall. On July 17, 1876, at War Bonnet Creek in Nebraska, troops under Colonel Wesley Merritt defeat Cheyennes under Yellow Hair and other chiefs. On September 9, 1876, at Slim Buttes in South Dakota, Crook defeats Oglala Sioux American Horse's band. On November 25, 1876, at Crazy Woman Creek in Wyoming (the Battle of Dull Knife), troops under Colonel Ranald S. Mackenzie defeat Dull Knife's and Little Wolf's Cheyennes. On January 8, 1877, at Wolf Mountain in Montana, Crazy Horse's followers attack troops under Colonel Nelson A. Miles. On May 7, 1877, at Muddy Creek in Montana (the Battle of Lame Deer), Miles defeats Miniconjou Sioux Lame Deer's band.

Nez Perce War (Flight of the Nez Perce): On June 17, 1877, at White Bird Canyon in Idaho, fighting breaks out between the Nez Perces under Chief Joseph and volunteers. On July 11, at Clearwater Creek in Idaho, the Indians outflank troops under General Oliver Howard. On August 9, at Big Hole in Montana, warriors under Looking Glass successfully counterattack the troops. On August 20, at Camas Meadows in Oregon, Nez Perce warriors launch a nighttime raid. On September 13, at Canyon Creek in Montana, the Indians again elude capture. On September 30–October 5, at Bear Paw Mountains in Montana, troops under Colonel Nelson A. Miles force a surrender of the refugees.

Bannock War: On July 8, 1878, at Birch Creek in Oregon, troops under Captain Reuben F. Bernard defeat Bannocks and Paiutes under Egan and Oytes (who replaced the fallen Buffalo Horn that June).

Ute War: On September 29, 1879, at the White River Agency in Colorado, Quinkent (Douglas) and other Utes kill Indian agent Nathan Meeker and nine of his employees. On September 29–October 5, 1879, at Milk Creek, militants under Nicaagat (Jack), Colorow (Colorado), and Canalla (Johnson) fight troops under Major Thomas T. Thornburgh, eventually retreating when reinforcements arrive under Colonel Wesley Merritt.

Apache Resistance: On October 15–16, 1880, at Tres Castillos in Mexico, Apaches under Victorio are defeated by Mexican troops.

Apache Resistance: On August 30, 1881, at Cibecue Creek in Arizona, the White Mountain (Coyotera) Apache shaman Nakaidoklini is killed by troops under Colonel Eugene Asa Carr. Geronimo, Naiche (son of Cochise), Chato, and other militants flee the San Carlos Reservation and head for Mexico. On April 19, 1882, Geronimo leads raid on reservation. On July 17, 1882, at Big Dry Walsh in Arizona, White Mountain Apaches under Natiotish are defeated. In March 1884, Geronimo returns to San Carlos. In May 1885, he flees the reservation again. On March 25, 1886, at Canyon de los Embudos in Mexico, Geronimo surrenders to General George Crook, but escapes again. On September 4, at Skeleton Canyon near Apache Pass in Arizona, Geronimo surrenders to General Nelson A. Miles.

Second Riel Rebellion: On March 28, 1885, Crees under Poundmaker attack the settlement at Battleford in Saskatchewan in support of the Metis cause. On April 2, Crees under Big Bear raid Frog Lake in Alberta. On May 9–12, at Batoche in Saskatchewan, the Metis under Louis Riel are besieged and eventually defeated by the North West Field Force.

Ghost Dance Uprising: On December 29, 1890, at Wounded Knee Creek in South Dakota, troops under Colonel James Forsyth attack the Miniconjou Sioux Big Foot's peaceful band, killing at least 150 men, women, and children (or perhaps twice that number) and wounding about 50 more.

GLOSSARY OF CULTURAL TERMS

activism Political and social action or involvement, sometimes militant. The term is applied to the philosophy and methods of 20th-century Indian individuals and organizations.

adobe A wet clay mixture, either sun-dried into bricks or applied wet as a mortar to bind stones, with straw sometimes added for strength; used in pueblo architecture.

allotment A U.S. federal policy, starting with the General Allotment Act (Dawes Act) of 1887 and lasting until 1934, in which tribally held Indian lands were broken up and distributed to individuals in 160-acre parcels to further assimilation and encourage private farming.

assimilation A U.S. federal policy of the late 19th and early 20th centuries, calling for the rejection of the tribal way of life and acculturation to Euroamerican customs.

atlatl (atl atl, dart sling, dart-thrower, spear-thrower, throwing stick, throwing board) A weapon that increases the leverage of the human arm to throw darts or spears; typically made from a stick about 16 to 20 inches long, with hide finger-loops for grasping, a stone weight for balance, and a groove and hook to hold the shaft of a projectile.

baidarka (baidarra) An Aleut boat, similar to the kayak of the Inuits, having oiled walrus or seal skins stretched over light wood frames. They were short, with the bow curved upward and the stern squared off; the bows were sometimes shaped like a bird's open beak. There were usually two cockpits, the rear one for the paddler, and the front one for the harpooner.

balsa A type of raft or boat made with bulrushes, especially of the tule plant, tied in bundles in a cylindrical shape. The bundles would become water-logged after a period of use, but would dry out in the sun. Some California Indians made balsas, as did some South American peoples.

band A subtribe (subdivision) of a tribe, often made up of an extended family, living, traveling, and obtaining food together. The word "band" often appears in historical text in reference to part of a tribe breaking off from a main group under a new leader. In Canada, different self-governing groups are referred to as "bands."

basketry (basket-making) The making of containers by interweaving plant matter, such as grasses, rushes, twigs, wood splints, roots, or bark; a textile art. The term is also sometimes applied to the making of bags, nets, mats, blankets, and wattle. True "weaving" typically involves the use of some support in the process, such as a loom. Feathers and beads are sometimes added to baskets for decoration.

bead A small, globular piece of some material, such as stone, clay, copper, wood, seed, bone, or horn, used for stringing on clothing, bags, and other items. Europeans introduced glass and porcelain beads to Indians, called "European beads." Beadwork designs have ornamental as well as symbolic and ceremonial purposes. Work with small pieces of shell and porcupine quills is generally referred to as "shellwork" and "quillwork."

Beringia (Bering Land Bridge, Bering Strait land bridge) During the Ice Age, because much of the earth's water was locked up in glaciers, the oceans were lower and more land was exposed. Where there is now water between Siberia (eastern Russia) and Alaska—known as the Bering Strait—there was once a land mass about a thousand miles wide, enabling travel between Asia and North America by Paleo-Siberians.

big-game hunting The hunting by Paleo-Indians of large, extinct mammals, such as bighorn bison, mammoths, mastodons, and saber-toothed tigers. Spears, atlatls, and stampeding techniques were used.

bighorn bison (longhorn buffalo) A now-extinct mammal, larger than and with longer horns than existing buffalo.

boarding school A school where Indian children were sent to live off reservations in order to further the policies of assimilation, especially in the late 19th and early 20th centuries.

booger mask A carved mask with exaggerated, often comical features; made by the Cherokees and worn in the Booger Dance during which tribal enemies are ridiculed. The name comes from the same European root as "bogeyman."

bow and arrow A bow is a weapon made from a curved strip of wood, bone, or horn (sometimes reinforced with sinew); strung with a bowstring (made from rawhide, sinew, gut or twisted vegetable fiber); and used to shoot a projectile. The projectile, or arrow, consists of an arrowhead, either wood or stone (and in post-Contact times, metal); an arrow-shaft of wood; arrow feathers (often from an eagle or turkey); and a nock (or notch) to fit on the bowstring. Arrow shafts were sometimes painted. Some shafts also had "lightning marks" or "blood grooves" cut along them, designed for preventing warpage, assuring straight flight, and allowing blood to flow from game.

buffalo (American bison, bison) A hoofed mammal (*Bison bison*) with a dark-brown coat and shaggy mane, heavy forequarters, large hump, and short curved horns. The primary habitat of the buffalo was the prairies and plains west of the Mississippi River and east of the Rocky Mountains. The buffalo was essential to the economy of the Plains Indians for food and materials.

buffalo skull The bleached skull of the buffalo, painted symbolically and stuffed with prairie grass, and serving as a sacred object during the Sun Dance.

bullboat A cup-shaped boat, made from hide, typically a whole buffalo skin, stretched over a willow frame and sealed with animal fat and ashes; used by Arikaras, Hidatsas, and Mandans for traveling and carrying supplies across the Missouri River and its tributaries.

calumet A Sacred Pipe, having special meaning for a tribe and used ceremonially. The term is most often applied to pipes of Great Lakes and Plains Indians with carved bowls of stone, antler, or bone, plus carved wooden or reed stems. Calumets are typically decorated with quills, beads, feathers, fur, or hair. "Calumet" is a French-derived word, meaning "reed" or "cane."

canoe A slender boat with pointed ends, propelled by paddles. The term usually refers to a frame boat with bark covering, especially birchbark, as made by Northeast Indians, but it is also used in reference to dugouts carved from a single log.

celt (ungrooved ax) A stone or metal tool with a wide blade, used for cutting and scraping in woodwork. Celts, unlike the heads of axes, have no groove for attachment to a handle, but some are thought to have been inserted in the cavity of a piece of wood or antler, or wrapped at one end in rawhide. Some celts served a ceremonial purpose.

chickee A Seminole dwelling, raised on stilts and open on four sides, with a wood platform and thatched roof.

Chilkat blanket A ceremonial blanket named after the Chilkat band of Tlingits, and made by them as well as by other Tlingit bands and by Tsimshians. The blankets were crafted from cedar-bark fiber and mountain-goat or mountain-sheep hair. Some of the yarn spun from wool was left white; the rest was dyed black, blue-green, or yellow to create "talking" designs.

Circum-Caribbean Culture Area A cultural and geographical region defined by scholars, comprising the West Indies; coastal Columbia and Venezuela in South America; as well as most of Honduras, Costa Rica, Nicaragua, and Panama in Central America. Arawaks and Caribs lived in the West Indies and in South America; many other tribes lived in the densely populated Central American part of the culture area.

cire perdue (lost wax) A technique of casting metalwork in which a clay model is covered in wax, then coated with an outer layer of clay and charcoal. The heating of the model causes the wax to melt, forming a space between the two ceramic layers, where molten metal is poured. After drying, the clay is removed, leaving a hollow metal object. To make a solid object, the model can be shaped of wax, then covered in clay; the molten metal takes the shape of the wax core, and the outer clay is removed after drying. *Cire perdue* is French for "lost wax."

city-state A city and its surrounding territory, having a government independent from other population centers; typical of the Mesoamerican Culture Area.

cliff-dwelling A dwelling along the walls of cliffs and canyons, located in the Southwest. Modification of natural caves and ledges was common through digging and the adding of stone or adobe walls. Wooden ladders provided access to the homes, grouped together for apartment-like living. Cliff-dwellings offered Anasazi and Sinagua peoples refuge from attackers.

code talker An Indian who used his native language to convey battlefield messages by radio for the military. Choctaw Indians acted as code talkers in World War I. In World War II, Choctaws again participated in Europe, as did the Comanches for the army's Signal Corps; Navajos created undecipherable codes for the Marines in the Pacific.

Columbian exchange The transfer of knowledge, technologies, peoples, plants, and animals, as well diseases, between the Americas and Europe (and by extension the rest of the world) during and after the voyages of Christopher Columbus.

contact A term, sometimes capitalized, used to describe the first meetings between Indian peoples and Europeans or Euroamericans. Pre-Contact refers to the period of time before Native Americans met whites, synonymous with pre-Columbian. Post-Contact refers to the period after which communication and trade were established. Contact for one tribe might have come at a different time than for another.

corn (Indian corn, maize) A cultivated plant of the Americas and the resulting edible seed (*Zea mays*), a cereal grass and staple crop of many tribes. Also called "maize" or "Indian corn," from the Arawakan *mahiz*. Corn was a staple for many tribes, and was celebrated in a variety of ceremonies, such as the Green Corn Festival of the Creeks.

coup stick A "coup" is an act of bravery in battle for Plains Indians, such as touching an enemy while he is alive with the hand, butt of a weapon, or a special stick, referred to as a "coup stick." "Counting coup" refers to the ceremonial recitation of deeds of bravery. *Coup* is a French-derived word for "blow" or "stroke."

disease Infectious illnesses brought to the Americas by Europeans played a large part in Indian history. It is estimated that tribal populations declined by about 10 percent from Indian-white warfare, but about 25 to 50 percent from diseases. Smallpox proved the most deadly disease because it returned time and again to the same populations, but measles, scarlet fever, typhoid, typhus, diphtheria, influenza, and chicken pox also took their toll. Contemporary Indians are known to have the poorest health care of any ethnic group, with a high rate of diabetes, tuberculosis, and other diseases.

Dog Soldiers (Dog Men, Hotamitaneo) A military society of the Southern Cheyennes, members of which drew power from dogs (and horses).

Dreamer Religion In the 1850s, the Wanapam Indian Smohalla, based on his dreams and visions, advocated traditional ways of life, free from white influences, such as alcohol and agriculture. Drawing on the teachings of other shamans, he established ceremonial music and dancing to induce meditation.

dugout A type of boat, made by hollowing out a log. Southeast and California Indians crafted small dugouts. Some Northeast Indians made boats in this fashion as well, in addition to their birchbark canoes. The large, seaworthy dugouts of Northwest Coast Indians were made from cedar logs; high bows and sterns were attached to hulls with cedar pegs and ropes, and totemic designs were then added.

earthlodge A large dwelling, about 40 feet in diameter, usually dome-shaped, with a log frame and covered with smaller branches, such as willow, or brush mats, then packed with mud or sod. Various eastern Plains tribes lived in earthlodges, such as the Arikaras, Hidatsas, and Mandans.

encomienda A Spanish term for a royal grant to conquistadors of Indian peoples for their tribute or labor, accompanying a grant of land. The policy amounted to legalized enslavement.

Euroamerican (Euro-American) A person from Europe living in the Americas, or a person born in the Americas of European ancestry; i.e., a non-Indian of European ancestry. The term is used synonymously with white in some writings.

Eurocentricism The tendency to view other cultures in terms of European culture and the belief in the inherent superiority of European culture. "Eurocentricism" is one form of "ethnocentricism," with Europeans and Euroamericans assuming that their form of progress and land development is superior to traditional Indian views. "Eurocentric" and "ethnocentric" are adjective forms.

False Face A mask worn by members of the False Face Society of the Iroquois Indians, representing a legendary being. They are carved from a living tree and are believed to give the wearer healing powers. The False Face Dance is performed by members of the False Face Society to heal the sick.

fish-in A type of civil disobedience in which Native Americans fish in waters, the use of which is banned by state or federal government, in order to demonstrate water rights as defined in treaties.

flaked stone tool (chipped stone tool) Any tool or weapon made by the process of "flaking," i.e. the removal of chips of stone, usually from chunks of flint, chert, or obsidian. In "percussion-flaking," the chips are removed by striking with a tool, usually a flaker of stone, bone, or wood. In "pressure-flaking," the chips are removed by applying pressure with a softer tool, usually of bone or antler.

fluting Grooves or channels in stone points. Fluting is made by removing a "channel flake." It is thought that the fluting was designed to fit to a shaft, and, in some cases, to facilitate deep penetration of game and increase the flow of blood.

fur trade Indians bartered animal skins and pelts for European manufactured goods, including iron tools, cloth, glass beads, firearms, and alcoholic beverages. The demand for furs was a driving factor in the European development of North America. The French, Dutch, English, Russians, and to a lesser extent the Spanish, developed an economy around the export of furs to Europe. French *voyageurs* and *coureurs de bois* traveled the wilderness in search of furs. Some tribes became partners in the enterprise: the Hurons acted as middlemen in trade with the French. The Aleuts were coerced into aiding the Russian fur traders (*promyshlenniki*). Fur companies were chartered to exploit this resource, and fortunes were made. Mountain men worked the Rocky Mountains. Much of the non-Indian exploration of the West resulted from activities of fur traders.

Ghost Dance (Spirit Dance, Ghost Dance Religion) A religious and cultural revival movement founded by the Paiute Indian Wovoka in 1889. Wovoka called for a return to traditional values and prophesied the disappearance of non-Indians and the return of the buffalo if certain rituals were performed, in particular "Ghost Dancing." While dancing, participants could supposedly catch a glimpse of this world-to-be. The movement spread throughout the West in the late 19th century, especially among the Sioux, who believed that special "Ghost Shirts" could repel bullets, leading up to the massacre of Indians by white soldiers at Wounded Knee in 1890.

grand sachem The leader of a confederacy of tribes. "Grand sachem" usually refers to a leader of an alliance; "sachem," to the leader of a tribe; and "sagamore," to a leader of subordinate rank within the tribe. "Sachem" is an Algonquian word, but it has also been applied to Iroquois chiefs.

grass house (grass lodge) A house covered with grass, typical of Caddos and Wichitas. Such a dwelling had long poles erected in a circle, usually 40 to 50 feet in diameter, with the tops meeting in a domed or conical shape; the framework was tied together, then covered with grass or thatch. Sometimes four doors were built in the direction of the cardinal points; or two doors, one facing east, to be used with the morning sun, and the other facing west, to be used with the afternoon sun.

high-steel Construction work on steel bridges and buildings. In 1886, Mohawk Indians of the Caughnawaga (Kahnawake) Reserve in Quebec were trained in high-steel construction to work on a bridge across the St. Lawrence River, starting a tradition among the Iroquois. Indian high-steel workers are contracted through their unions for work all over the world. They are sometimes called "skywalkers."

hogan A Navajo dwelling with a log and stick frame covered with mud or sod (or sometimes made from stone). Usually one-roomed, it can be cone-shaped or dome-shaped, six-sided, or eight-sided. It traditionally faces east. The original Navajo word for house or hut in the Athapascan language is *goghan*.

horse The horse native to the Americas became extinct at the end of the Ice Age. Later generations of Indian peoples did not have knowledge of the animal until the arrival of the Spanish. As Spanish colonies spread out from the West Indies and Mexico, so did the horse (*Equus caballus*), used for transportation. Pueblo Indians took care of herds for colonists along the Rio Grande. During the Pueblo Rebellion of 1680, hundreds of the animals fell into Indian hands. Some horses also went wild and were tracked down. Trade in horses spread northward onto the Great Plains. Use of the animal was widespread by the end of the 18th century, with Indians of many tribes proficient as breeders, trainers, and riders.

Ice Age A geological era characterized by the alternate advancement and recession of glaciers over what is now ice-free land. The Pleistocene period was the most recent ice age, or series of ice ages with interglacial periods (interstadials). When capitalized, "Ice Age" refers specifically to the Pleistocene.

igloo (iglu, snowhouse) A dome-shaped dwelling of the Inuits, made from blocks of ice; typically 9 to 15 feet in diameter and sometimes with an additional room connected by a passageway. Snowhouses were used only by the Central Eskimos and only in the winter.

Indian Territory A tract west of the Mississippi River, set aside as a permanent homeland for Indians in 1834 (after originally being defined as the "Indian Country"), including much of present-day Nebraska, Kansas, and Oklahoma, then diminished over the following years. In 1854, with the Kansas-Nebraska Act, the northern part became Kansas and Nebraska territories. In 1862, the Homestead Act opened up many remaining Indian lands to white homesteaders. In 1890, Oklahoma Territory was carved out of much of it. In 1907, the twin territories of the remaining Indian Territory and Oklahoma Territory together became the State of Oklahoma.

Iroquois League (Iroquois Confederacy, Great League, The Great Peace) An alliance of tribes, made up, east to west, of Mohawks, Oneidas, Onondagas, Cayugas, and Senecas, founded about 1570 by the Mohawk Indian Hiawatha (Heowenta) and the Huron Indian Deganawida (The Peacemaker). The confederacy is also referred to as the "Five Nations," and, after the early 1700s, when the Tuscaroras out of North Carolina joined, as "Six Nations." The Iroquois native name is *Haudenosaunee* for "People of the Longhouse."

kachina (katchina) A supernatural being in the religion of the Hopis, Zunis, and other Pueblo Indians. The many different kachinas have varying characteristics and represent different animals, plants, or forces of nature, in particular rain; or they represent ancestral beings. Kachinas supposedly stay in the other world for half the year, and move invisibly among human beings the other half. The beings are impersonated by men wearing "kachina masks" and costumes. "Kachina dolls" are given to children to instruct them in tribal religion. In the Uto-Aztecan language of the Hopis, *kachina* means "spirit-father."

kiva An underground ceremonial house of the Pueblo Indians, a kind of pithouse, serving as a sacred chamber and clubhouse. Kivas are usually circular in shape, and sometimes built partly above the ground with stone or adobe. A ladder provides entrance through a flat roof; inside are found a firepit, an altar, and a *sipapu*, a hole in the floor, symbolizing the center of the universe and passage to the Spirit World, through which the first humans emerged, the deceased pass, and legendary beings come and go.

lacrosse A game played with long-handled rackets, goals, and a small ball. The game in its original form was a sham battle for the Iroquois, Choctaws, and other eastern Indians. Lacrosse is now played all over the world.

language Spoken communication distinct in vocabulary, grammar, and phonetics. A "dialect" is a variation of a particular "language." A "language family" or "linguistic stock" refers to two or more languages, distinct but with elements in common and assumed to be descended from a common language. A "language phylum" or "linguistic superstock" is a grouping of language families, based on elements in common, including vocabulary, grammar, and phonetics. A "language isolate" is a unique language with no recognizable elements in common with other languages. The classification of Indian languages is inconclusive and theoretical because of the fact that so many languages are extinct. It is estimated that 1,800 to 2,200 different languages were spoken by native peoples in the Americas at the time of early contacts with Europeans: 200 to 300 north of Mexico, 300 to 350 in Mexico and Central America, and the rest in South America.

ledger art (ledger drawing) A representational drawing showing an incident in the life of an individual, often in pencil or crayon, typically on the page of a ledger (record) book. Many Plains Indians, especially Cheyennes, Comanches, and Kiowas, imprisoned at Fort Marion in Florida during the 1870s, filled ledger books with their drawings.

longhouse A long dwelling, with a pointed or rounded roof and doors at both ends, made with a post-and-beam or bent sapling frame, and covered with slabs of elm bark. The Iroquois and Hurons lived in longhouses, which were divided into compartments for different families with raised platforms for sleeping. Some Algonquian tribes built longhouses as council houses.

Longhouse Religion In 1799, the Seneca Indian Handsome Lake, alcoholic and sick, experienced a series of visions after which he began advocating self-purification through traditional rituals and lifeways. He also encouraged the values of family, community, and modern agriculture, emphasizing the centrality of land to the tribe. His beliefs came to be defined as the Code of Handsome Lake. The term "Longhouse Religion" is applied to both traditional Iroquois religious practices and as a synonym of "Handsome Lake Religion."

Long Walk A historical event which occurred in 1864 during the Navajo War, when Navajos were forced by white troops to relocate from what is now eastern Arizona and western New Mexico to a reservation at Bosque Redondo near Fort Sumner in eastern New Mexico. Hundreds of tribal members died during and after the march.

mammoth A large, now-extinct mammal of the genus *Mammuthus*, similar to the elephant. Mammoths were once common on the grasslands of North America and were hunted by Paleo-Indians. The "wooly mammoth" was one variety.

mask A covering worn on the face and sometimes head. Indian masks are used ceremonially, symbolizing animal spirits or legendary beings, and are thought to give the wearer power. Some masks are made from animal heads; others are crafted from wood, basketry, pottery, hide, or ivory, and painted and decorated with a variety of materials. Some masks have two or more faces. The making, handling, and storing of masks are all ritualized.

mastodon (mastodont) A large, now-extinct mammal of the genus *Mammut* (or *Mastodon*). Mastodons were browsing animals resembling elephants, living in forested as well as grassland regions, and hunted by Paleo-Indians. Paleontologists distinguish them from the similar mammoths by their molars.

Mesoamerican Culture Area (Mesoamerica, Meso-America) The geographical name of a cultural and historical region, including most of Mexico, except the northern part, which is included in the Southwest Culture Area; all of Guatemala, Belize, and El Salvador; and parts of Honduras, Nicaragua, and Costa Rica. Mesoamerica, sometimes referred to as "Middle America," was a densely populated region, where some people developed city-states and highly structured societies. At the time of first contacts with whites, the Aztecs were the dominant civilization of the region.

Midewiwin Society (Grand Medicine Society, Mide Cult) A medicine society of the Chippewas and other Great Lakes Indians and eastern Sioux. The sodality, i.e. club, was organized around four lodges into which members were inducted. The initiates sponsored feasts and in return were instructed in the secrets of myths and sacred animals, as well as in the rituals of healing and the medicinal properties of plants. *Midewiwin* translates as "mystical doings" or "spirit doings" in the Chippewa dialect of Algonquian; the Potawatomi spelling is *Midawiwin*.

mission A body of persons sent to do religious work in a region; also, the religious center established there. Missions in Indian lands consisted of churches and schools and were centers of operation for missionaries of many different denominations. Jesuits,

Franciscans, Congregationalists, Presbyterians, Episcopalians, Methodists, Quakers, and other groups. The phrase "Mission Indians" refers to those Indians forced to give up their tribal way of life and live at missions; it is most often applied to California peoples missionized by the Spanish. Eastern Indians were more often referred to as "Praying Indians" or "Christian Indians."

Morning Star Ceremony Pawnee Indians of the Skidi band believed that the Sun and Mother Earth conceived the Morning Star, the God of Vegetation. Once a year, the Skidis would raid another tribe for a young girl in her early teens. They would keep this girl among them for months, honoring her. In the early morning of the summer solstice, priests would paint the girl red for day, and black for night, then tie her to a rectangular frame in a field outside the village, where she was sacrificed as the morning star rose. In the early 1800s, Petalesharo, who would later become principal chief, rallied his people against the cruelty of the ritual and the power of priests.

mound An earthwork. Mounds were used for burials ("burial mounds"); as effigy figures ("effigy mounds"); or to hold temples or houses ("temple mounds"). Other mounds were made as enclosures and fortifications. The term is also sometimes applied to shell-heaps and other middens (refuse heaps). The Indians of the Adena, Hopewell, and Mississippian cultures are referred to as "moundbuilders."

Native American Church A religious revitalization movement, founded in 1918 by followers of the Peyote Way, that incorporates Christian beliefs, such as non-violence, with the sacramental use of peyote. The Native American Church, in resisting a number of legal attempts to suppress the use of peyote, has played a central role in the Indian struggle for freedom of religion.

paddle A wooden implement, wide at one end. The term is applied to boat paddles, as well as to corn and acorn mush paddles used in food preparation.

parfleche A storage bag used to hold clothing, ceremonial objects, or meat, made from rawhide with the hair removed. The rawhide itself is also called "parfleche."

peyote A type of cactus (*Lophophora williamsii*), native to northern Mexico and the American Southwest. Peyote buttons, the plant's dried blossoms, are ingested for spiritual and healing purposes. The hallucinogenic effect is considered a channel for prayer by members of the Native American Church. "Peyote" is a Spanish word, derived from the Nahuatl *peyotl* for "caterpillar," in reference to the appearance of the button's downy tuft. Peyote is also sometimes called "mescal," a name for the agave plant.

pictograph (pictogram) A picture or sign representing a word or idea (not representing a sound, as in alphabet-writing). Native Americans carved pictographs in wood, bark, shell, and stone; painted them on hide; and tattooed them on the human body. Color in pictographs had symbolic meaning as well. The term "pictography" is synonymous with "picture writing." The terms "hieroglyphics" and "glyph writing" are also sometimes used interchangeably with "pictography." "Pictograph" and "ideograph" ("ideogram") can be synonyms; the latter is sometimes used in reference to a series of concepts as opposed to a representation of one event.

pipestone (catlinite) A type of stone, pale grayish red to dark red, sometimes mottled, soft enough to carve pipe bowls. The alternate term "catlinite" is named after frontier painter George Catlin, who visited and wrote about the Pipestone Quarry in Minnesota, a sacred site where many tribes came for pipestone.

pithouse (semisubterranean house) A dwelling erected over an excavated hole. To construct a pithouse, a structure, usually made with a post-and-beam frame with walls and roof of saplings, reeds, earth, mats, or skins, is placed over a shallow pit. Plateau Indians lived in pit houses, as did Indians of the Hohokam and Mogollon cultures.

plank house A rectangular dwelling of the Northwest Coast Indians, made of planks, usually cedar, over a log frame. Totem poles were sometimes structural parts of plank houses.

point A spear point or arrowhead; also referred to as a "projectile point." Points were made out of stone, bone, antler, and, in post-Contact times, metal.

potlatch A ceremony in which possessions are given away or destroyed for the sake of prestige. Northwest Coast Indians sponsored potlatches to celebrate weddings, dedicate new houses, or raise totem poles, or for other rites of passage. The ceremony included feasting, speechmaking, singing, and the giveaway. Blankets were a common gift. The term is derived from the Nootka word *patshatl* for "sharing."

pottery Objects of fired clay, or the making of such objects; a technology used to make containers, pipes, utensils, effigy figures, toys, and other objects. Native American pots were originally molded without a wheel, or shaped by means of coiling, in which ropelike coils of clay were built up from the bottom, then smoothed over.

powwow (powow, pauwau) A social gathering and celebration, including feasting, dancing, and singing, prior to a council, a hunt, or a war expedition; or the council itself. Modern-day powwows have elements of both fairs and festivals, with arts and crafts on display and open to non-Indians; a "contest powwow" offers prize money for dancing. The term is from the Algonquian language, originally meaning "he dreams" or "he uses divination," in reference to a shaman.

Praying Indians (Christian Indians) Christianized Native Americans. The term is used especially in reference to New England Indians, in particular to some among the Massachusets, who were converted by the Protestant missionary John Eliot, beginning in 1646. Their settlements, such as Natick, became known as "praying villages." The term "Mission Indians" is more often applied to California peoples.

pueblo The Spanish word for an Indian village; used in a reference to the villages of certain Southwest Indians. Pueblos have apartment-like architecture, made from adobe and wooden beams, up to to five stories high, with the different levels connected by wooden ladders. Entrance to homes is through hatchways in the roofs. In addition to communal houses, pueblos have kivas and plazas. The term "Pueblo Indians" refers to Hopis, Zunis, and Indians of the Rio Grande pueblos.

pyramid A massive stone monument, with a rectangular base and four sides extending upward to a point, as found in the Mesoamerican Culture Area as well as in ancient Peru. Native

American pyramids, the tallest of which was about 140 feet high, were built in a series of superimposed platforms, and were used to hold temples.

quillwork Work in porcupine quills. Quillwork is found on clothing, bags, pipes, and other items. The shafts of bird feathers were also utilized. Quills were softened in water or the mouth; flattened by drawing them through the teeth, or with a rock or bone tool; colored with dyes; and applied as a form of appliqué on various materials, especially animal skins.

rattle A musical instrument that makes percussive sounds when shaken. Some rattles have small objects, such as pebbles and seeds, in a hollow container, made from rawhide, wood, gourds, turtle shells, hooves, and horns, sometimes with a handle attached. Other rattles are made from two objects of about equal size that make a rhythmic noise when coming in contact; pods, shells, bird beaks, and other materials have been used in this design. Still other rattles have a number of small objects, such as hooves, claws, or teeth, strung together. For most tribes, rattles were sacred objects, sometimes called "medicine rattles" or "spirit rattles," to be used by shamans. In the sign language of the Plains Indians, the sign for "rattle" was used to indicate "sacred."

relocation The forced or encouraged removal of Native Americans from one location to another. A common governmental practice in the 19th century, when eastern tribes were relocated to the Indian Territory. From the early 1950s into the 1960s, the federal government sponsored a modern relocation and assimilation policy, encouraging Indians to move from reservations to cities.

removal A policy formalized with the Indian Removal Act of 1830, in which U.S. and state governments forced eastern tribes to leave their ancestral homelands and move west of the Mississippi River to the Indian Territory.

repartimiento A Spanish grant of lands to individuals, along with the right to impose an annual levy for labor and produce on some among the native population. The *repartimiento* system replaced the *encomienda* system in 1542 and lasted throughout the remainder of the Spanish colonial period.

repatriation The reacquisition by a tribe of human remains or sacred objects from the government, museums, or private owners, as defined in the Native American Graves Protection and Repatriation Act of 1990.

reservation A tract of land set aside historically by the federal or a state government for occupation by and use of Indians, based on treaty negotiations. Reservations were formerly used to restrict Indians to specific territory; they now are tribally held lands with a special protected status. In California, the term "rancheria" is also used; in Canada, the term "reserve" refers to protected tribal lands.

reserve The Canadian equivalent of a reservation. In Canada, different bands (tribal entities) usually have more than one reserve tract of land.

ribbonwork A kind of patchwork or appliqué in which silk ribbons are sewn in strips on a dress. Also called "ribbon appliqué," "silk appliqué," and "rickrack."

saber-toothed tiger (saber-toothed cat, sabertooth) Any of various extinct mammals of the cat family, especially of the genera *Machairodus* and *Smilodon*, equaling the tiger in size, but with long, curved upper canine teeth; hunted by Paleo-Indians.

sacred site A location with special historical or mythological meaning for a tribe. Such natural places include mountains, lakes, rivers, streams, caves, and rock quarries. Man-made places include burial grounds, mounds, rock piles, and rock art.

Sand Creek On November 29, 1864, Colorado volunteers under Colonel John Chivington attacked peace chief Black Kettle's encampment of Southern Cheyennes and Southern Arapahos at Sand Creek near Fort Lyon in Colorado, killing about 200 men, women, and children. The Sand Creek Massacre, like the Trail of Tears, the Long Walk, and the Wounded Knee Massacre, has come to symbolize the suffering of Indian peoples.

sandpainting A design made by trickling colored sand onto plain sand for ceremonial purposes; a ritual practiced by the Navajos.

scalping The cutting or tearing away of a circular patch of skin and hair from the top of the human head. Scalping is one of those customs which has mistakenly come to be associated with all North American Indians. Scholars disagree on just how widespread the practice was before the coming of whites, or if it were practiced at all. In any case, the custom became common after various wars of the 17th and 18th centuries during which French, Dutch, and English officials placed a bounty on Indian scalps, because they were easier to transport than heads.

self-determination A tribal and governmental policy calling for Native American self-government and economic self-sufficiency, along with cultural renewal.

Shaker Religion In 1881, the Squakson (Coast Salish) Indian John Slocum founded Tschadam, known to whites as the Indian Shaker Religion, named after the shaking or twitching motion participants experienced in meditation while brushing off their sins. The religion combined Christian beliefs with traditional Indian rituals.

shaman A mediator between the worlds of spirits and humans. A shaman interprets and attempts to control the supernatural in order to bring success in food gathering and warfare and to cure the sick; he also is keeper and interpreter of tribal lore. The religious functions and political power of shamans varies among tribes, with some also acting as chiefs. "Medicine man" is a synonym.

shield A defensive weapon, worn on the arm to ward off attack. Plains and Southwest Indians made shields of rawhide stretched over a wooden frame and usually painted. Ornaments, especially feathers, were added. A shield was considered a sacred possession by Plains Indians ("Sacred Shield"), its design determined in dreams. Some Pueblo Indians crafted shields out of basketry. Eastern Indians were known to make them from bark or woven willow. The Aztecs had shields covered with feather mosaics.

slavery Slaveholding, or the keeping of people as property, was practiced by a number of tribes in pre-Contact times, especially among Mesoamerican Indians and Northwest Coast Indians, who carried out slave-raids on other tribes. In post-Contact times, some among the wealthier Southeast Indians kept black slaves, as their white neighbors did. Some tribes, such as the Seminoles, adopted runaway slaves into their families. The taking of slaves provided economic impetus for European exploration and development of the Americas, starting with the voyages of Christopher Columbus.

sled (sledge) A vehicle, drawn by people or dogs, used for carrying people or possessions over snow and ice. A sled has runners and a raised platform. The use of sleds was widespread among the Inuits, and among some Subarctic Indians as well. Many modern-day Inuits have given up the dog sled in favor of the snowmobile.

soapstone (steatite) A kind of stone with a soapy texture, gray, green, or brown in color, a variety of talc; soft enough to be carved with stone tools, but which hardens with exposure to air. Soapstone has been used to make bowls, pipes, ornaments, and ceremonial objects. Contemporary Native American sculptors, especially among the Iroquois, work in the material.

Sun Dance An annual renewal ceremony among Plains Indians, as well as some Plateau Indians and Great Basin Indians, in which a vow was fulfilled to a sun deity. The ceremony lasted 8 to 12 days. The various Sun Dance rituals involved drumming, singing, dancing, and self-torture. One particular ritual has come to be associated with the entire ceremony above all others: some men had skewers implanted in their chests muscles, which were tied to a sacred pole with ropes; they danced backwards for hours until the skewers ripped through their flesh; while others dragged buffalo skulls about the camp with similar skewers. The Arapahos called it "Offerings Lodge," and the Cheyennes, "New Life Lodge."

syllabary A list of symbols, each one representing a syllable (in a true alphabet, a symbol represents a single sound). The "Cherokee alphabet," invented by Sequoyah, was a syllabary of the Cherokee language for writing.

tepee (teepee, tipi) A conical tent of Plains Indians, having a pole frame and covered with buffalo hides. A tepee has 13 to 20 poles, averaging 25 feet in length. The circular base is typically 15 feet in diameter. At the top, there is a smokehole; adjustable smoke flaps allow the smoke from a central fire-pit to escape. The door is a piece of hide, stretched on a pole or on a hoop and traditionally facing east. The ground serves as the tepee's floor; in the winter, grass is added around the bottom for insulation. A dew cloth or tepee liner also provides insulation. Three or four beds are situated along the wall on either side of the door and opposite. Tepees are often painted or decorated with ornaments. The word consists of the Siouan roots *ti*, "to dwell," and *pi*, "used for."

termination A U.S. federal policy of the late 1940s to the early 1960s, that called for the end of the special protective relationship (trust responsibility) between the government and Indian tribes, transferred much of the responsibility for Indian programs to states, and induced relocation to urban areas.

thanksgiving The ritual expression of gratitude, often for a successful harvest or successful hunt or catch. Many tribes had thanksgiving ceremonies, which involved feasting. In 1621, the Pilgrims shared a thanksgiving feast with the Wampanoags, who had enabled them to survive by teaching them how to plant corn and use fish as a fertilizer. The custom was adopted as a U.S. national holiday.

Thunderbird A legendary being, prevalent in the tradition of Northwest Coast Indians, but found in other traditions as well; sometimes represented as an eagle. When the Thunderbird flies, the flapping of its wings supposedly creates thunder and the blinking of its eyes creates lightning.

tobacco Any of various plants of the genus *Nicotiana*, especially *N. tabacum and N. rustica*. Native Americans considered tobacco a sacred plant and used it in many rituals, some of them for purposes of healing. It was smoked in pipes or in its own leaves; eaten; snuffed; burned as incense; sprinkled in the air; or tied in a small bundle and placed on an altar. In less than a century after Europeans first reached the Americas, the use of tobacco circled the globe, making its way to Alaska via Europe and Asia. The word "tobacco" is derived from the Arawakan word *tabaco*, a cigar-like roll of tobacco leaves.

toboggan A vehicle for transporting people or possessions over snow or ice. Toboggans, unlike true sleds, have no runners; their platforms are directly on the snow. Subarctic Indians used toboggans. An Algonquian word, meaning "what is used for dragging."

tomahawk (tomahack, tomahog) A type of warclub. "Tomahawk" is an Algonquian word referring to a variety of stone or wooden clubs, used as tools or weapons (both hand weapons and missiles). In popular usage, the term has come to refer to a weapon with an iron head, made by Europeans, i.e., a "trade tomahawk." Those which doubled as pipes are called "pipe-tomahawks" and were used ceremonially.

totem pole A wooden post, carved and painted with a series of figures and symbols, having meaning with regard to tribal history and legends. Some totem poles stand alone; others are structural parts of a plank house. Northwest Coast Indians carved totem poles from cedar. Some Eastern tribes erected smaller poles for use in medicine lodges.

Trail of Tears The forced removal and journey of the Cherokee Indians from their homelands in the East to the Indian Territory. In 1830, President Andrew Jackson signed the Indian Removal Act to relocate the eastern tribes west of the Mississippi River. Although the principal chief of the Cherokees, John Ross, argued against forced removal before the Supreme Court of the United States and won, the decision was ignored. Soldiers began rounding up Cherokee families and taking them to internment camps in preparation for the journey westward. With little food and unsanitary conditions, many Cherokees died. The first forced 800-mile journey began in the spring of 1838 and lasted into the heat of summer. The second mass exodus took place in the fall rainy season, when the wagons bogged down in the mud, and in the winter of 1839, during freezing temperatures and snow. The Cherokees suffered from exposure, inadequate food supplies, disease, and attacks by bandits. During the period of confinement, and the two trips, about 4,000 Cherokees died, a quarter of those relocated. More Cherokees died after arrival in the Indian Territory because of continuing shortages of food and epidemics. Other tribes endured similar experiences, including the Chickasaws, Choctaws, Creeks, and Seminoles, also in the 1830s, and the "Trail of Tears" has come to be symbolic for the forced removals of all Indian peoples.

treaty A formal agreement between two or more political entities, that is between the federal government (or state, provincial, or territorial governments) and Indian tribes as sovereign nations. Treaties define terms of peace, including such issues as political control, boundaries, land sale, restitution, and trade.

tribe A general term applied to different kinds and degrees of social organization. Tribes usually have language, culture, kinship, territory, and history in common, and are comprised of a number of bands or towns. The term generally implies political and economic equality among tribal members. In the modern legal sense, a distinction among tribes is made among tribes that are federally recognized, state-recognized, or self-recognized; some are organized as corporations, as in the regional and village corporations of Alaska. Some tribes refer to themselves as "nations"; others, as "communities." The term "band" is used in Canada for tribal entities. The word "tribe" is derived from the Latin word *tribus*, a division of the Roman people.

trust relationship A tribe's special relationship with the U.S. government, unlike that with any other political or economic group, resulting from federal recognition. The federal government has the responsibility, based on treaties, statutes, and court cases, to recognize, protect, and preserve tribal sovereignty and guarantee the transfer of resources.

wampum Beads made from shells, especially the dark purple (or black) and white quahog clam shells. Algonquian and Iroquoian tribes used the shell-beads as ornaments; they also used "wampum belts" (or sashes or strings) as tribal records and to communicate messages to other tribes. In post-Contact times, Native Americans began making wampum out of glass beads. The Europeans also made wampum for trade purposes, and it became a medium of exchange. "Wampum" is a shortened version of *wampumpeag*, an Algonquian term meaning "white strings."

warbonnet A type of Plains Indian headdress with different feathers, typically the black-tipped tailfeathers of the male golden eagle, symbolizing deeds in battle. The making of warbonnets was a ceremonial event. The feathers were attached to a skullcap of buffalo or deerskin, with a brow-band that was decorated with quillwork or beadwork and dangling strips of fur or ribbons. Additional downy feathers were tied to the bases of the eagle feathers and tufts of dyed horsehair to their tips.

warclub A club designed as a striking weapon. Some warclubs are single pieces of wood, such as the ball-headed club, or pieces of bone or antler; others have heads attached to handles. In post-Contact times, iron was also used for one or more pointed heads. There were numerous designs, some handles shaped like a rabbit's hind leg or in the "gunstock" style. The "tomahawk" is a kind of warclub.

wattle-and-daub A type of construction in which a pole framework is intertwined with saplings and vines then filled with mud or clay. Southeast and Southwest Indians built such dwellings.

wickiup (wikiup) A dome-shaped, conical, or triangular dwelling of the Apaches and Paiutes, with a pole frame covered with brush, grass, reeds or mats. Probably an Algonquian word, from the same root as wigwam. The term has been applied to any brush shelter.

wigwam A dome-shaped or conical dwelling of Algonquian Indians in the Northeast, having a pole frame (bent-frame construction) covered with bark, woven mats, or hide. Usually built over a shallow pit, with earth piled around the base. Wigwams have holes in the top to let out smoke. An Algonquian word, meaning "dwelling." The term has been applied generally to dwellings of non-Algonquians as well, as an equivalent of "lodge."

winter count A calendar of pictographs, recording a tribal event for the period from spring to spring, or one year. Plains Indians, especially the Kiowas and Sioux, drew winter counts on buffalo and deer hides, and, in post-Contact times, on pieces of canvas, cotton, or muslin.

Wounded Knee The name of a creek in South Dakota and an event in Indian history on December 29, 1890, that has come to symbolize the end of the Indian wars, the cruelty to native peoples, and the continuing struggle for justice. During the Ghost Dance movement in the West, white officials became alarmed at renewed Indian militancy and banned the ritual on Sioux reservations and ordered the arrest of key leaders, among them the Miniconjou chief Big Foot. Big Foot, ill with pneumonia, sought only peace. He led his band, most of them women and children, to Pine Ridge to join up with the neutral Oglala chief Red Cloud, not with the Ghost Dancers Kicking Bear and Short Bull. An army detachment under Major S. M. Whitside intercepted Big Foot's band and ordered them to set up camp at Wounded Knee Creek. Then Colonel James Forsyth arrived to take command of the prisoners. The next morning, Forsyth sent in troops to collect all Indian firearms. A medicine man named Yellow Bird called for resistance, saying that the Ghost Shirts would protect the warriors. When the soldiers tried to disarm a deaf Indian named Black Coyote, his rifle discharged in the air. The soldiers shot back in response, eventually with heavy artillery, killing men, women, and children alike. At least 150 Sioux (and possibly twice that number) died unnecessarily at Wounded Knee, with many more injured. In honor of their ancestors and in protest of the broken treaties by the federal government and the lack of opportunity for Native Americans, members of the American Indian Movement (AIM) staged an occupation at Wounded Knee in 1973. The incident ended in violence, with two Indians, Frank Clearwater and Buddy Lamont, killed by federal agents.

CAPTIONS AND CREDITS

TITLE PAGE

Chippewa cone-shaped birchbark wigwam.

CULTURE TIMELINE

1492	Arawak stone sculpture of Death's Head.
1492-93	European compass rose from early map.
1540	Arapaho leather and bead toy horse.
1560-70	"The Pacification of Atotarhoh" by Jesse Cornplanter, Iroquois, 1906. (Deganawida and Hiawatha form the Iroquois League.)
1564-65	Archaic Indian point.
1587	Painting by John White
1600	Sheep motif. Santa Fe Collection.
1608	Painting of Pocahontas. Courtesy of Library of Congress.
1613	Beothuk birchbark canoe.
1643	"Roger Williams Sheltered by the Narragansetts." Courtesy of Library of Congress.
1661	Pueblo Indian kiva.
1675	Chippewa quillwork container.
1700	Chippewa Midewiwin water drum.
1722	Iroquois clay pipe.
1750	Iroquois false face.
1760-63	Lenni Lenape interior post for a ceremonial house.
1769	California Indian dwelling, with tule over a framework of poles.
1769	Luiseno basket.
1780	Fox courting flute.
1780	Fox ribbonwork dress.
1799	Iroquois longhouse.
1809-21	Sequoyah, with his syllabary of the Cherokee language. Courtesy of New York State Library, Albany.
1817	Pawnee skull symbolizing the First Man.
1820	Etowah Mound, Georgia. Photo by Molly Braun.
1824-30	Mohongo, an Osage woman, and child. Painting by Charles Bird King, 1830. Courtesy of Library of Congress.
1833-34	Blackfoot Indian by Karl Bodmer. Courtesy of National Archives.
1843	Inuit mask symbolizing the Soul of the Salmon.
1848	Haida whale rattle.
1850	Otter motif. Dover Publications.
1853	Navajo silversmith, 1880. Courtesy of National Archives.
1875	Crayon sketch by Howling Wolf, Cheyenne, 1876.
1879	Mythical motif. Santa Fe Collection.
1883	"Buffalo Bill" Cody and Native American friends. Courtesy of Library of Congress.
1884	Chinook bowl made from the horn of a bighorn sheep.
1885	Cheyenne buffalo effigy pipe bowl.
1889	Sioux Ghost Shirt.
1889	Pueblo Indian pottery.
1897	Haida dugout.
1897	Chilkat blanket with "talking" designs.
1900-30	Edward Curtis and Native American friends. Courtesy of Library of Congress.
1910	Sioux Sun Dance buffalo skull.
1911	Yahi glass arrowhead made by Ishi.
1911	Rabbit motif. Santa Fe Collection.
1912	Jim Thorpe. Courtesy of National Archives.
1917	Inuit mother and child in Nome, Alaska. Courtesy of National Archives.
1918	Comanche drum for peyote ceremonies.
1936	Gros Ventre leather and beadwork pouch.
1936	Ute basket.
1936	Zuni pin.
1936	Seminole doll.
1940	Detail of Navajo sandpainting.
1957	Nootka salmon headdress.
1960	Zuni dance wand.
1961	Painting of Cornplanter. Courtesy of Library of Congress.
1969	Kiowa pin.
1978	Kwakiutl totem pole.
1978	Menominee calumet.
1979	Cheyenne shield, taken by George Armstrong Custer at the Battle of Washita.
1987	Fish motif. Santa Fe Collection.
1989	Kwakiutl wooden mask of Spirit of the Sea with killer whale.
1990	Crow ceremonial rattle.
1991	Plains Indian buffalo hide tepee.
1991	Cheyenne pipe.
1993	Mohawk soapstone turtle.
1993	Mohawk ash-splint and sweetgrass basket.
1993	Bella Coola eagle mask.
1994	Sioux eagle feather warbonnet.

WARFARE & PROTEST TIMELINE

1493-95	Arawak stone celt.
1519-21	Aztec clay figurine.
1519-21	Aztec sacrificial knife.
1519-21	Aztec shield with feather mosaic.
1540	Coushatta alligator basket.
1613	Micmac birchbark moose call.
1622	Southeast Indian blowgun and dart.
1622	"Powhatan's Mantle." Hide decorated with shells, thought to have belonged to Chief Powhatan.
1675-76	Wampanoag warclub, thought to have belonged to Metacom (King Philip).
1680	Hopi kachina doll.
1680-83	Yuchi wand for the Feather Dance.
1688-1724	Abenaki bow and arrow.
1689-87	Chippewa warclub in "rabbit's hind leg" style.
1695	Pima basket with labyrinth design.
1729	Natchez effigy pipe.
1720-52	Algonquian birchbark canoe.
1744-48	Abenaki cone-shaped wigwam.

1760-61	Arrow motif.
1761-66	Aleut baidarka.
1775-83	Painting of Joseph Brant (Thayendanegea). Courtesy of New York State Library, Albany.
1775-83	Seneca cornhusk mask.
1790-94	Miami warclub in "gunstock" style.
1802-05	Tlingit knife of ivory, leather, and iron.
1808-39	Beaver motif. Santa Fe Collection.
1813-14	Creek wattle-and-daub dwelling.
1819-33	Kickapoo prayer stick with carved symbols.
1819-33	Kickapoo wigwam.
1824	Detail of Chumash rock art.
1825	Pomo elkhorn knife.
1835-42	Osceola. Painting by George Catlin. Courtesy of Library of Congress.
1847	Pueblo architecture.
1850-51	Yokuts balsa (tule raft).
1851	Mojave Indian, 1871. Courtesy of National Archives.
1851	Mojave effigy jar.
1854-57	Sioux warclub.
1858	Plateau Indian warclub.
1860	Paiute wickiup.
1860	Toad motif. Santa Fe Collection.
1863	Bear motif. Santa Fe Collection.
1863-65	Painting of Manuelito. Courtesy of National Archives.
1864-65	Arapaho shield.
1867	Arapaho ceremonial coup stick.
1869	Metis knife.
1872-73	Apache wickiup.
1874-75	Kiowa ceremonial lance.
1876-77	Sioux tree burial. Courtesy of National Archives.
1876-77	Crow bow.
1878	Arrow motif.
1881-86	Geronimo. Courtesy of New York Public Library.
1881-86	Snake motif. Santa Fe Collection.
1890	Bigfoot. Courtesy of National Archives.
1901	Snake motif. Santa Fe Collection.
1912	Central Inuit igloo.
1912	Tlingit girl, 1903. Courtesy of National Archives.
1914-18	Pima Indian Ira H. Hayes, Pfc., Marine Corps. Courtesy of National Archives.
1958	Seminole chickee.
1968	Chippewa rattle.
1968	Iroquois false face.
1969-71	Tsimshian bow.
1971	Plains Indian Sacred Pipe.
1973	Sioux shield.
1975	Plains Indian Sacred Hoop.
1990	Kahnawake Reserve, 1990. Photo by Molly Braun.
1994	Leonard Peltier, "Dream Seeker." GlengaDesign.

POLITICS & LAW

1512	Aztec rhythm instrument made from a human bone.
1512	"Las Casas Bewailing the Cruelty of the Spaniards." Hypothetical gravure, 1801. Courtesy of Library of Congress.
1512	Arawak gold frog.
1521	Aztec turquoise and shell pendant.
1582	Archaic Indian point.
1584	Algonquian wigwam.
1626	Two European pipe-tomahawks for trade with Indians.

1636	Algonquian birchbark canoe.
1638	Algonquian wampum.
1643	Mohegan wooden doll.
1663	Feather motif. Santa Fe Collection.
1754	Iroquois wampum.
1768	Massachuset wooden bowl.
1775	Iroquois lacrosse stick.
1778	Lenni Lenape drumsticks.
1790	Flathead digging stick.
1790	Northwest Coast Indian Thunderbird.
1790-99	Algonquian canoe.
1802	Mandan earthlodge.
1803	Hidatsa bullboat.
1827	John Ross. Courtesy of Library of Congress.
1831-39	Cherokee booger mask.
1845	Eagle motif. Santa Fe Collection.
1850	Chippewa cone-shaped wigwam.
1851	Sioux parfleche.
1854	Wichita grass house.
1860	Kootenay birchbark canoe.
1862	Hidatsa hoe, with shoulder blade of elk.
1864	Navajo hogan.
1864	Mythical motif. Santa Fe Collection.
1867	Plains Indian tepee.
1867	Haida paddle.
1867	Tlingit screen for the facade of a plank house.
1868	Blackfoot eagle headdress.
1869	Athapascan toboggan.
1869	Naskapi mask.
1870	Kwakiutl spoon.
1876	Haida whistle.
1884	Inuit sled.
1885	Detail of Navajo sandpainting.
1891	Miwok mush paddle.
1917-20	Northwest Coast shaman's Spirit Helper.
1924	Apache boy. Courtesy of National Archives.
1932	Bird motif. Santa Fe Collection.
1948	Laguna Pueblo, New Mexico. Courtesy of National Archives.
1948	Navajo mask.
1951-52	Arapaho drumstick with quillwork eagle design.
1961	Rock on Kahnawake Reserve. Photo by Molly Braun.
1969	Yakima cornhusk bag.
1973	Menominee arrow.
1974	Snake motif. Santa Fe Collection.
1974	Hopi kachina.
1994	Deer motif. Santa Fe Collection.
1994	Cree pipe bag.

ARTWORK ON MAPS

Northeast:	Abenaki birchbark canoe.
Southeast:	Seminole chickee.
Southwest:	Zuni dance mask.
Great Basin:	Washoe basket.
Plateau:	Wishram skeleton figure.
California:	Diegueno basket.
Northwest Coast:	
	Makah raven mask.
Great Plains:	Cheyenne buffalo robe.
Famous Battles:	Sioux arrow.

Motifs: Santa Fe Collection. Clip Art. Copyright © 1990-92 RT Computer Graphics.

BIBLIOGRAPHY

(General titles for further reading and research)

Axelrod, Alan. *Chronicle of the Indian Wars: From Colonial Times to Wounded Knee.* New York: Prentice Hall, 1993.

Baity, Elizabeth Chesley. *Americans Before Columbus.* New York: Viking, 1961.

Ballantine, Betty, and Ian Ballantine, eds. *The Native Americans: An Illustrated History.* Atlanta: Turner Publishing, 1993.

Bear, Leroy Little, Menno Boldt, and J. Anthony Long, eds. *Pathways to Self-Determination: Canadian Indians and the Canadian State.* Toronto: University of Toronto Press, 1984.

Berkhofer, Robert E. *White Man's Indians: Images of the American Indian from Columbus to the Present.* New York: Random House, 1979.

Bierhorst, John, ed. *The Sacred Path: Spells, Prayers, and Power Songs of the American Indian.* New York: William Morrow, 1983.

Billard, Jules B., ed. *The World of the American Indian.* Washington, D.C.: National Geographic Society, 1979.

Brandon, William. *Indians.* New York: American Heritage; Boston: Houghton Mifflin, 1985.

Brown, Dee. *Bury My Heart at Wounded Knee: An Indian History of the American West.* New York: Holt, Rinehart, and Winston, 1970.

Burland, Cottie. *North American Indian Mythology.* New York: Peter Bedrick Books, 1985.

Catlin, George. *North American Indians.* New York: Viking, 1989 (reprint of 1841 text, edited by Peter Matthiessen).

Ceram, C.W. *The First American: A Story of North American Archaeology.* New York: Harcourt Brace Jovanovich, 1971.

Coe, Michael, Dean Snow, and Elizabeth Benson. *Atlas of Ancient America.* New York: Facts On File, 1986.

Collins, Richard, ed. *The Native Americans: The Indigenous People of North America.* New York: Smithmark, 1992.

Cornell, Stephen. *Return of the Native American: Indian Political Resurgence.* New York: Oxford University Press, 1988.

Debo, Angie. *A History of the Indians of the United States.* Norman, OK: University of Oklahoma Press, 1977.

Deloria, Vine, Jr. *Custer Died for Your Sins: An Indian Manifesto.* Norman, OK: University of Oklahoma Press, 1988.

_____. *God is Red.* New York: Dell, 1973.

Dockstader, Frederick J. *Great North American Indians: Profiles in Life and Leadership.* New York: Van Nostrand Reinhold, 1977.

_____. *Indian Art of the Americas.* New York: Museum of the American Indian, Heye Foundation, 1973.

Driver, Harold E. *Indians of North America.* Chicago: University of Chicago Press, 1969.

Eagle/Walking Turtle. *Indian America: A Traveler's Companion.* Santa Fe: John Muir Publications, 1991.

The Editors of American Heritage. *The American Heritage Book of Indians.* New York: American Heritage, 1961.

Embree, Edwin R. *Indians of the Americas.* New York: Macmillan, 1970.

Fagan, Brian. *The Great Journey: The Peopling of Ancient America.* New York: Thames and Hudson, 1987.

Fey, Harold E., and D'Arcy McNickle. *Indians and Other Americans: Two Ways of Life Meet.* New York: Harper & Row, 1970.

Fiedel, Stuart J. *Prehistory of the Americas.* Cambridge: Cambridge University Press, 1987.

Fleming, Paula, and Judith Luskey. *The North American Indian in Early Photographs.* New York: Harper & Row, 1986.

Gibson, Arrell Morgan. *The American Indian: Prehistory to the Present.* Lexington, MA: D.C. Heath, 1980.

Gonzalez, Ray. *Without Discovery: A Native Response to Columbus.* Seattle: Broken Moon Press, 1992.

Hagan, William T. *American Indians.* Chicago: University of Chicago Press, 1979.

Hausman, Gerald. *Turtle Island Alphabet: A Lexicon of Native American Symbols and Culture.* New York: St. Martin's, 1992.

Highwater, Jamake. *Arts of the Indian Americas: Leaves from the Sacred Tree.* New York: Harper & Row, 1983.

_____. *The Primal Mind: Vision and Reality in Indian America.* New York: New American Library, 1981.

_____. *Ritual of the Wind: North American Ceremonies, Music, and Dance.* New York: Van Der Marck, 1984.

_____, ed. *Words in the Blood: Contemporary Indian Writers of North and South America.* New York: New American Library, 1984.

Hirschfelder, Arlene, and Paulette Molin. *The Encyclopedia of Native American Religions.* New York: Facts On File, 1992.

Hirschfelder, Arlene, and Martha Kreipe de Montano. *The Native American Almanac: A Portrait of Native America Today.* New York: Prentice Hall, 1993.

Hodge, Frederick Webb, ed. *Handbook of American Indians North of Mexico.* 2 vol. Washington, D.C.: Bureau of American Ethnology, 1907–1910.